CREDIT WARFARE

Retake Control of Your financial Life!

ISBN-13: 978-1475191141
ISBN-10: 1475191146

TABLE OF CONTENTS

INTRODUCTION

In the early 1990s we experienced a recession not quite as bad as the great recession but painful for many nonetheless. Back then I did live radio five nights a week on this one subject (credit) broadcast out of Miami. The program, like this book, was called *Credit Warfare* and focused each night on a new credit or debt issue. Many people listened nightly on their ride home from work. It was the highest rated program on AM radio during drive time because so many people needed help.

Doctors, lawyers, judges, secretaries, police officers, nurses, truck drivers etc… listened to *Credit Warfare* and used the information to pull their lives back together. A superior court judge became a federal judge. A police lieutenant became a captain. Others got new jobs and started businesses. They were now able to get the best rates on insurance, homes, cars, credit cards and so on because they were trained to handle their credit / debt business themselves.

Then the internet explosion came and with it millions of jobs. People started to feel like things were getting better and went back to spending money without worrying about how they would pay the bills if another recession came along.

Fast forward to 2003 when the housing boom really took off. 68% of you owned, bought or refinanced homes and with that came the purchase of everything to go in it. We leveraged ourselves to the hilt thinking this modern "gold rush" would never end.

Fast forward again to 2008. The wheels fell of the proverbial bus. Foreclosures, defaults, law suits, bankruptcy and so on became the new norm for millions of Americans. 20 years have passed and a new generation is experiencing the pain of the greatest recession since the 1930s.

As I write this book more than 61 million Americans have bad credit with another 30 – 40 million classified as bruised to sub-prime. I knew things were getting bad back in 2007 when I started receiving emails from those who listened to me on the radio or came to my seminars 15 years earlier asking for help again.

As was the case then, you can re-take control of your financial life without a credit repair company, credit counseling or in most cases an attorney. You can stop the creditors, collectors and lawyers with little effort and regain some sense of serenity in very short order if you know what your rights are and how to enforce them. You truly can remove any negative information from your credit report on your own with minimal time invested.

Credit Warfare will provide you with the knowledge you need backed up with legal references, resources, a plan of action and step by step instruction to deal with any credit or debt collection issue regardless of whether you are a novice or experienced consumer. Most importantly this book will help you sleep at night knowing you have the power to fix the issues at hand legally and protect yourself from further attack.

I taught thousands back then how to fight back and rebuild their lives. This book is fully updated based on amendments to the relevant laws and new case law covering every issue from debt collection to creditor rights.

I encourage you to use the tools within these pages to educate yourself and start getting your life back together.

As my mom used to say … *"One miracle at a time"*

ABOUT THE AUTHOR

S. Louis Blisko is a noted expert on credit and debt collection issues. He has written hundreds of articles over the past twenty five years on the subject and the challenges presented to individual Americans and our economy as a whole. He was the host of *"Credit Warfare"* a two hour radio program heard weeknights for nearly six years for which this book was named.

Americans of every sort tuned in to the program using his research and strategies to rebuild their lives after being victims of natural disasters, job loss, crimes, business failure, medial and other issues they could not have foreseen or planned for.

He has taught attorneys, accountants, financial planners, real estate and insurance professionals about credit and debt collection strategy to better assist their clients, solve financial problems and recover from financial crisis.

He is the fifth of five children with three older sisters and a brother and has been married for seventeen years with one child of his own.

PREFACE

For decades we have relied on credit to live our version of the American dream. We leverage everything we buy. Particularly the larger ticket items like education, cars and houses but in the 2000s we went further leveraging cell phones, services, furniture, vacations, dental work, cosmetic surgery and more.

This terrible habit of financing (leveraging) everything we want while making the foolish assumption our income will remain as is or increase forever put our country in its most vulnerable state since the 1930s. When the bottom fell out in 2008 we were in collective shock. There we were with our oversized homes, expensive cars, platinum credit cards, perfect smiles and technology wondering what on earth happened and what do we do now?

Few of us were trained for a scenario like this. No courses in high school or college prepared us for economic collapse. No information was passed on by our families to show us how to deal with collection agents, falling credit scores and potential foreclosure. We spent and spent as we were told to do trusting in the idea our economy was on a roll and wouldn't stop. Wars, deficits, deregulation, greed and a blind eye could all be blamed equally but none of it matters much now does it?

Now we want to know how to get out of it. Never mind getting back to the luxury life we were living; we'll take just one month of no collection calls, steady income of some type and a few decent nights' sleep. How about a weekend where you don't fear Monday coming? While our politicians berate each other for everything but the weather we sit wondering when this nightmare will end. When will life feel "normal" again?

Some people blame others when things go wrong financially. They wait for someone else to solve their problems while the rest of us get up, get educated and work toward a solution. Now is one of those times where if we wait for others to bring us back from the depths we'll be waiting a very long time. It's time to take responsibility for ourselves. To get educated and form a plan of action that leads each one of us to a sustainable recovery; but how? Where do we begin? What information do we need to take the first steps?

Credit Warfare was designed to answer these questions in great detail giving you a guideline to fix the problems keeping you up at night while forming a plan of action to fully recover both credit wise and psychologically.

This isn't a time for the faint of heart. Rebuilding our lives takes determination, toughness, education, personal responsibility and most of all action. There are many books available attempting to tell you how the credit system works and how to "repair" your credit. None go as deep or provide the resources, references and tools you'll find here.

Credit Warfare gives you the power to retake control of your financial life using the law, tactics and strategies designed to put you in a position of strength. This book was specifically designed to make you capable of taking action that will give you almost instant control over your financial life where previously you thought you had lost it to creditors pouncing for money. You'll find detailed legal strategies that cost nothing but teach you how to control everything such as stopping collection agents, repairing your credit and forming a plan to full recovery and future insulation.

Credit Warfare provides the resources you need to not only rebuild your financial life but to make sure you never end up in the same situation again.

CREDIT REPORTING – Behind The Curtain

Most Americans are accustomed to buying things they want by leveraging them. That is, we sign our name and a company or "creditor" guarantees the payment on our behalf. The "creditor" (bank, retail store etc...) relies on another type of company called a "credit bureau" to provide a snap shot of our history in order to decide whether or not to extend credit to us in the first place.

Credit bureaus make their living receiving information about our financial habits and history, then selling the information to others who are considering extending credit to us. It's important to remember these credit bureaus are not divisions of the government. They are a business like any other and must abide by rules, regulations and laws like any other business. Many of you may think these companies are the government and as a result are hesitant to confront them when they misreport or make unfair character references.

Before you embark on this most important mission to retake control of your financial life and restore your credit to a favorable standing, there are some important facts you should be aware of.

First, you are not alone. Consider the following. According to a recent Nilson report, there are roughly 172 million credit files with enough data to generate a credit score. 25% or approximately 43 million credit reports contain serious errors. 75% or approximately 130 million contain an error of some type. 61 million Americans have subprime credit scores (Between 500 – 649).

Think about it; 61 million of your fellow Americans cannot get approved for an unsecured credit card, low interest mortgage or car loan. If you take into account those other Americans with scores between 649 and 680 (preferred minimum score for credit card) you add at least another 25 million people. The Great Recession has definitely taken its toll.

It took some time for you to get into this situation; you'll need to allow a reasonable amount of time to get out. The saying goes, "a journey of a thousand miles begins with a single step". *Credit Warfare* teaches you how to form a strategy to first put the fires out, to create a safe zone for you to live inside of and last to recover and restore your financial life.

"Know Thy Enemy and Know Thy Self" *Sun Tzu*. By this we mean you must first understand how the bureaus and collectors run their business and how to deal with them on terms they understand and respond to. Second you need to know yourself in terms of what your weaknesses are and how to strengthen yourself to avoid them in the future. So let's begin by introducing you to your enemy. Pay attention now because every piece of information somewhere along the line connects with another piece of information which if used correctly leads to financial serenity and a cleared credit report.

Remember, this program is designed to help those who through some unfortunate circumstance experienced financial difficulties. It is this author's opinion that one should not be punished for seven or ten years simply because you went through a tough time. Better than 90% of you had something happen that wasn't within your control such as being laid off, serious illness, injury, natural disaster, business failure, market changes and failures, divorce and even crime.

It is unfair to punish people by in effect black listing them without also demonstrating they were financially sound for many years before the incident causing their financial downturn. A system that punishes a person for pulling their life back together and paying off their debts by leaving the negatives on their credit report for seven additional years from the point they pay the debt off is an unbalanced system. This imbalance leaves us with no other option but to learn what our rights are and fight back with the same set of rules the credit bureaus and collection companies use.

Now then; your enemy has three heads. They are (Equifax, Experian & Trans Union). They are not the same company but are the same adversary. Your enemy is in business to make money, not to help you. They make money by selling information about you to whoever presents a "legitimate business need". We'll get to that later.

For now remember there are dozens of credit bureaus in the United States. For the most part they all feed off the "Big Three" Equifax, Experian and Trans Union. The "Big Three" gross billions of dollars each year selling our credit information to individuals and companies most often without our knowledge or consent. Your enemy doesn't care if your credit report is accurate or inaccurate. They make the same money either way.

Your enemy is not in the debt collection business, at least when they're acting as a credit bureau. They are not interested in how much money you owe or why you owe it. Your enemy doesn't care if you paid the account off, the account was settled and released or any other explanatory statement you may think is a valid reason for the information to come off your report.

Your enemy will use any explanation you give them for your difficulties to keep the accounts you feel should be removed on your report for another seven years. (i.e. 100 word statement)

Your enemy receives its information by selling memberships to companies who offer financing or other products and services requiring a credit check. The average charge for this service to corporations is about $3.00. For you it's free annually and $8.00 or more per bureau thereafter.

In exchange for the privilege of being able to pull a credit report on someone, each company agrees to report any data good or bad on every customer they have back to the credit bureau regularly. This is how credit bureaus get their information, not by seeking it out *aggressively* but by receiving it *passively*.

As a result of their passiveness they are considered by the courts to be nothing more than a *conduit* of information. Just like a tabloid magazine, they can print anything about you as long as someone else says it's true. They don't need to check with you because of another clause in the law "reasonable procedures to insure maximum possible accuracy" which we'll get to later. It's critical for you to understand how they get their information in order to understand how to remove the negative accounts from your credit reports. Write this down, "Credit Bureaus Do Not Search Public Records"

They would like you to believe they are connected by computer somehow to every court house in the United States and every Judgment, Bankruptcy, Tax Lien, or other legal action comes to their immediate attention by virtue of their incredible ability to procure and process this information instantaneously.

Do you know how many courthouses there are in the United States? How about how many individual cases are filed in all of those courthouses every day? No courthouse in the country is a subscriber of any credit bureau nor do they make any effort to cooperate with them. They have enough work to do. The last thing they see as a priority is helping the credit bureaus.

So how then does the credit bureau get that information? Simple, the creditors involved in each instance report the case (judgment, foreclosure, tax lien, bankruptcy) to the bureau. This is their only real means of collecting money or in the case of Bankruptcy their last chance to lash out at you for filing and having the debt discharged. Yes that's the only way the credit bureau knows about a Bankruptcy.

The same thing applies to any of the other type of information mentioned earlier. In other words it's the IRS collection division who tells the credit bureau you have a tax problem, not the court the lien was filed in.

Ok, so now you know how the credit bureaus get information. There are a few other things you should know about credit reporting you probably didn't know.

1. **Any** person or company who is a "**member**" or customer of any credit bureau **can report anything** they want about you whether it is true or not because the credit bureau has no legal responsibility to investigate it until you make a request for re-investigation (i.e.; Atlanta case where racial epithet is placed on Equifax report by auto sales co.)

2. **Without being diligent** and checking your report on your own **you won't know** to make that request because in addition to the above statement the bureau is also not obligated to notify you if a company reports negative information about you in the first place (FCRA sec.609 - no mention).

They will however be happy to sell you a monthly service to "monitor" your credit for you and notify you of these items. I recommend pulling your reports yourself at least twice per year. It will be cheaper, does not affect your score and you get it instantly.

3. Any company with a "legitimate business need" (FCRA Section 604:3f) can pull your credit report and cause an inquiry to appear and stay for years without your written authorization.

4. The credit bureaus make the same money whether your credit report is good or bad so they have no real incentive to want to help you except upon your letting them know that legally they have no choice. Remember, they are corporations and are only interested in the bottom line. You won't get much cooperation without pushing a bit.

5. By their own admission, no credit bureau will guarantee to us or to any of their corporate customers the information contained in any consumer file is in fact *accurate*. Yet they sell this information like a commodity to the tune of billions of dollars a year and our financial lives depend on them every day. **You must correct your credit reports with all three major bureaus** because you never know which one or combination of bureaus a company may use. For instance, Experian is the largest of the three and is mainly used on both coasts and by most major corporations.

Equifax on the other hand is primarily used in the southeast and some major corporations. Trans Union is concentrated in the mid-west and southeast, but very few major corporations use them as a primary source.

Correcting one bureau and not the others will only result in a lesson in futility. Why? Not every company you ask to extend credit to you uses the same source for credit reports. Although each credit bureau concentrates in certain areas of the country, they overlap as well. Additionally, potential creditors may and often do, check in more than one place before deciding whether or not to extend credit to you. Generally the larger the purchase or amount being financed the further and deeper they check.

Just a few years ago the credit bureaus sent out a press release stating that they will be able to resolve disputes in one day (USA Today). They also stated that if information is removed from one credit bureau the other two would follow suite. This was obviously in response to the tremendous pressure being brought on by consumer groups around the country. Sources inside the bureaus told me at the time that even if the bureaus were sincere, the earliest this change would have taken place would be years. It never happened.

Of course we now know it was just another publicity stunt aimed at calming what they perceived to be rough seas while legislation was in motion. However, the FCRA has been amended for the third time in 41 years. We'll discuss the changes later. The most recent changes went into effect in October of 2001 and somewhat revised in 2004 when the "F.A.C.T Act" was added. The new law defines most of the ambiguous clauses found in the old one. More needs to be done but the most recent changes were a good start.

Many attempts were made over the decades to amend the FCRA but the opposition was so strong and the support so weak it died before even reaching the full committee. For example, in 1994 one senator (Phil Graham rep. Texas) all by his lonesome stopped the law from being amended more than once.

He argued if you were able to get a copy of your credit report for $3.00, it would bare too much of a financial burden on the smaller credit bureaus. Of course what he didn't consider is that the small credit bureaus are specialty bureaus for mortgages, cars, apartments etc. and charge the companies who use them a large fee ($15.00 to $75.00) for pulling summary reports. Nor did he consider that the smaller bureaus get their information from the big three.

So if they have no file on you there is no cost and if they do it's because somewhere along the line they were paid handsomely to prepare a report on you for someone else.

Fortunately the people prevailed and the FCRA was in fact amended in 1997, 2001 and most recently in 2004. The new law strengthens the strategies discussed in this book. It clears up many issues and yet still leaves some to be dealt with. There is still some ambiguity but for the first time key issues have been made clear.

We'll discuss them in detail later. So the consumer must learn to defend themselves against unfair credit practices but how? Nowhere in the country is there a comprehensive source of information that lays out step by step how to correct negative credit reports without leaving huge gaps in the strategy.

Yes there are books in book stores, libraries and free pamphlets from the FTC, but none of them actually tell you the mechanics of what you need to do and how exactly to do it until now of course. *Credit Warfare* was designed to fill those gaps.

Your investment in this book will serve you for the rest of your life. The information contained herein is based on more than 20 years of experience and research. If you read from beginning to end you will be able to solve any credit or collection problem you have legally and in a relatively short period of time. I know what you're thinking, why is he telling me this now I already bought it? The answer is simple.

Everyone wants very badly to get their situation straightened out. So sometimes, and **I'm not saying *you* would ever do this**, people go straight to the sample letters in the back of this book as if they were the cure for cancer.

However, the sample letters are meant to be nothing more than a guideline for most situations so you can get started quickly. If you don't know which legal strategy to apply to your problem you may just shoot yourself in the foot. So please take the 90 minutes or so required to read through the book and educate yourself, you'll be glad you did and so will your foot.

On the next page is a short test that may anger you a bit but hopefully will peak your curiosity further. Take a few minutes and write down the best answer you can think of. No! The answers are not all in one place in the back of the book, you guessed it; they're spread throughout the full text. Now you have to read the whole thing.

CREDIT WARFARE – Test Your Knowledge

1) Does negative information automatically come off your credit report after a certain period of time?

Circle One -   YES   NO

A] How long?   3yrs   5yrs   7yrs   10yrs

B] At what point does the time period begin? (Underline one)

(When debt is charged off) (Date last paid) (Date of last activity) (Date account was reported) (180 days after charge off date)

2) How long does Bankruptcy remain on your report?

 5yrs   7yrs   10yrs   15yrs

A] How long do the accounts included in the BK stay?

5yrs   7yrs   10yrs   15yrs

B] How long does a withdrawn or dismissed BK stay on?

5yrs   7yrs   10yrs   15yrs

3) Do you have to pay the debts before they can come off your report?

Circle One - YES   NO

4) How long can a collection account stay on your report?

A] until you pay   B] 7yrs   C] indefinitely

5) How long does the credit bureau have to investigate a dispute?
A] 30dys   B] 60dys   C] 90dys   D] indefinitely

6) The credit bureau's computer identifies you by which?

A] ss#   B] ss# + lst name   C] ss# + lst nm + address

D] ss#,lst nm, address, date of birth   E] all of the above

7) Is it illegal for a sales person to show you your credit report?
Circle One - YES   NO

8) Can a creditor or collection agency remove negative information from your credit report if they choose to?

Circle One - YES   NO

9) Can a company pull your credit without written authorization?

Circle One - YES   NO

 10) Does removing information from your credit report absolve you of the debt?

Circle One   - YES   NO

11) Do credit bureaus search court documents to acquire info?

Circle One - YES   NO

12) Will paying the debts off in full restore your credit standing?
Circle One - YES   NO

How well do you think you did on the test? Well fear not, this is only the beginning. The idea is to test yourself until you are familiar with all of the information. Remember the questions are answered throughout the book so read on and take notes. You don't want to get a "0" do you? What would your parents think?

FREE CREDIT REPORT – 5 Different Ways

Obtaining your credit report is easy and something you should do at least once a year (I recommend 2 times per year). You have every right to know what's being reported about you. Just imagine if your bank didn't send you a statement every month. You would be outraged and rightly so. You should have the same attitude about your credit reports. At least once a year you should know where you stand credit wise. So make it a habit to keep a current copy on hand.

Pulling your own reports also helps keep inquiries to a minimum. You show the creditor (bank etc..) a current copy of your report pulled by you and instruct them to give you a preliminary answer / approval for your application without pulling a copy of their own yet.

Once you decide whom you want to do business with you can let them pull a copy for themselves. That will keep the inquiries to a minimum. Car dealerships are notorious for creating multiple inquiries on credit reports by sending the application out to several banks.

Section 610 of the Fair Credit Reporting Act (FCRA) states under what circumstances you may obtain a copy of your credit report. First of all, you may either get a copy in person, over the phone, through the Internet or by mail upon presenting the credit bureau with proper identification. You may also have someone else obtain a copy on your behalf as long as you provide a letter authorizing the bureau to release and / or discuss your file with that person.

Section 612 of the FCRA says if you have been denied credit because of a report generated by any bureau, that bureau must provide you with a copy for free.

There are several other reasons you may be entitled to a free copy of your credit report.

1. Free Annual Report – You are entitled to copy of your report once per 12 month period at no charge.
2. If you have been "made aware there may be adverse information" on your report you have a right to a report for free. So if you receive a letter regarding a debt or a phone call for all intents and purposes you have been made aware.
3. If you are Unemployed and intend to apply for employment in the 60 days following your request for the report.
4. If you are a recipient of public assistance
5. If you have reason to believe your credit file contains inaccurate information due to fraud.

To get your free annual credit report you can go online to http://www.annualcreditreport.com . The site will ask a few questions and then provide access at no charge.

Experian will provide a report and score for $1.00 on their web site. Equifax offers a report and score on their web site for $15.95 and Trans Union (worst of the three) tries to sell you a monthly membership for $16.95 per month. You do NOT need this.

Instead follow these directions to get your Trans Union Report.

1. On TransUnion.com scroll down on the home page.
2. Under the "Consumer Assistance" section click the link for the "Fair and Accurate Credit Reporting Act"
3. On the next page next to the text saying "You may be eligible for a credit report at no charge or reduced fee" click the "Expand All" button and then scroll down.

4. Under "Negative Credit History" heading click the link saying "Purchase a TransUnion Credit Report"

5. On the next page click "Register" under "Create an Account".

6. Fill out the form and then they charge you $11.00 for 1 Report and Score.

Check our web site (www.creditwarfare.com) for updated information if you need it. Remember the system at each bureau has changed so you must have a copy of your report before they will get on the phone and discuss it. You can do it online so don't wait. Once you have a copy of your report each bureau provides an 800# for you to call and speak to a human. Remember to be very careful in what you say should you call and discuss the disputes with them.

Credit bureau addresses and phone numbers can be found in the reference section of this book.

CREDIT REPORTS – Demystified

Ok, so now you have a copy of your report. There are several different dates, graphs with check boxes and sections all looking like a big maze of information.

Actually it's simple. The reports are sectioned off by categories. Usually there is a report "summary". Next would be personal information like the way our name appears, any alias they have, social security number(s), phone numbers, spouse and job. Then there are sections for public information (judgments, tax liens, bankruptcy) and Inquiries.

There will be a section for "Negative Items". These would be the accounts which are showing as late, charged off, foreclosed etc... Credit accounts come in three varieties. "R" which stands for revolving accounts like credit cards you only need to pay a portion of the balance each month.

"O" means that the account is open, usually one that is paid in 30 days like American Express. "I" stands for installment account, which could be used for student loans, mortgages and cars. The letter defines what type of account it is, not how good or bad the payment history is.

When viewing negative or positive accounts the account name comes first followed by the account number, date it was opened, how many months it has been reported, date of last activity or date last reported, high credit, terms, balance, and status. It's the status we need to be concerned with.

The status could show as "paid" or "paid as agreed", 30 days, 60 days, 90 days, CO or Charged Off, CLS or Closed Account and "C" or Collection Account. Try and keep your emotions in check when reviewing your reports. Emotion doesn't help resolve the issues.

The *date of last activity* was the last time the creditor reported any information on that account. *High credit* means the original amount of the loan or the highest balance the account has ever been reported with in the case of a credit card.

There is one more thing you should pay attention to. Underneath the account it will show if any late payments have ever been made. They list these in little boxes or columns representing months within a given year. Each is either marked with "Ok" or a number (30, 60, 90) representing you were late and exactly how late the account was at that time. Just in case the format is confusing they usually provide an explanation sheet or "legend" either accompanying the report, at the top of it or on the back.

Each report will show you an area of how many potential negative items there are and how many positive items. They will also give you the inquiries broken down as those which will be seen by a potential creditor and those which won't.

Some inquiries are not allowed to be shown on reports sold to those with whom you apply such as inquiries created by a company that checked your credit just to see if they wanted to extend an offer to you.

All three of the credit bureaus include with the report a dispute form received by U.S. mail or one presented online. They tell you to fill out the form and send it in or submit it to them so they can "better assist you". Oh they'll assist you; after you fill out their form the way they want you to, you would most likely have given them information they weren't entitled to (we'll get to that later). For now remember, do not use their form.

If you look at it for a moment it looks like a multiple choice quiz. The problem is most of the choices guarantee you'll fail, so **don't use it** until at minimum you have read this entire book and understand how careful you need to be when doing so.

On every credit report there is a section for the accounts and then there are three other sections you will need to look over. The first shows all of the "Public Record" information like (judgments, bankruptcies, tax liens, & child support). The second is usually titled "Additional Information".

This is where they put previous address, employer, & spouse. The last is for listing "Inquiries", which represents every time a company or individual pulled a copy of your credit report.

When you look at the Public Records section it will show what type of case it was, when it was filed, who filed it, and for how much. **Pay close attention to this information** because it becomes critical later. It will also show the (alleged) current disposition of the case.

In other words it will note if the case has been settled, dismissed, withdrawn, paid, satisfied, discharged or unpaid. Again, this is critical to note in order to decide how to proceed.

With respect to the accounts listed on the top section of the report such as, credit cards, car loans, mortgages, student loans etc., they may have a disposition underneath them as well. It could read, Collection Account, Charged Off, Paid, Satisfied or Closed Account. Most of these are self-explanatory. For the sake of clarity let's go over them.

A "_Judgment_" is when a lawsuit was filed against you and the plaintiff won, either by "default" meaning there was a hearing and you didn't show, or by trial. A "_Bankruptcy_" is a petition you file for yourself (usually with assistance from counsel) in federal court stating you cannot pay the debts and are asking for "relief" from those obligations.

It is a Federal Case, meaning all Bankruptcies are filed in federal court and are based on federal law. A "_Tax Lien_" is a judgment for money allegedly owed in taxes. It can be either, Federal or State. "_Child Support_" appears when you have gone through a divorce and were supposed to pay it and did not.

A "_Settled_" account is one that you worked out an arrangement to pay an agreed sum prior to a trial or judgment. "_Dismissed_" means either the court decided at trial you were in the right, or the Plaintiff (Creditor) never showed up. "_Withdrawn_" means that the Plaintiff asked the court to disregard / withdraw their complaint. "Dismissed" could also mean, in the case of a bankruptcy you did not show for the hearing. "_Paid_" & "_Satisfied_" mean just that. You either paid off the court judgment or paid off the collection account. "_Discharged_" means that you filed a bankruptcy and the court discharged or relieved you from paying the debts.

There are two remaining things you should look over. They are the balances on each account and your personal information i.e. name, address, social security number, and date of birth to be sure they are accurate.

You see, when you apply for credit the creditor makes their decision to lend based on several criteria. One of which is your "debt to income ratio". Simply put, this is a formula to determine your gross income vs. what gets paid out for bills. The magic number is a 2 to 1 ratio.

They want to see you take in two net dollars for every one you pay out. So check the balances and be sure your ratio is correct. Lastly, as silly as it sounds to the rest of us, check your report to be sure they show the correct personal information. Otherwise your report will have alias's on it.

What is that you ask? Well, every time you apply for credit or someone pulls your credit report they have to put in your primary information to get the computer to locate your file. If by accident they should mistype something like your name or social security number it creates an "Alias" on your report. Even though this was through no fault of your own, it is usually viewed as a negative by future creditors. The implication is that you might deliberately be trying to use multiple names, addresses etc… to trick the system. Nonsense!

NOTE: Do not correct the personal information until all of the negatives have been removed. See *The Two Point Match* chapter for details.

Remember, those credit reports are the only thing standing in the way of you moving on with your life. Don't be foolish enough to just blow through it and end up making a major mistake. Looking them over will only take a few minutes and they are a few minutes well spent.

THE FAIR CREDIT REPORTING ACT – Discussion

The "Fair Credit Reporting Act" is the Federal Law that sets the guidelines protecting us from unfair representations of our financial character by creditors, collectors and credit reporting agencies. It was enacted in 1970 after Congress realized these companies had tremendous power over our financial lives. Unfortunately at the time Congress couldn't possibly have conceived of how large a problem this would become 42 years later.

The FCRA lays out the rules of play regarding credit reporting and the methods discussed later of how to legally remove negative information from your credit report.

There are several sections of this law that provide a way to legally remove negative information. The first is Section 611. This section is titled "Procedure in case of disputed accuracy," and provides the most common method for dispute. Most importantly it gives us the legal right to dispute something regardless of the alleged status of the account.

Section 611 says **any** information in your report which is found to be "inaccurate" or "can no longer be verified" must "promptly" be deleted from your credit report. This same section also says the bureau has "30 days beginning on the date on which the agency receives the notice of the dispute from the consumer" to re- investigate and record the current status of the information

In 1997 congress for the first time in 27 years amended the FCRA. They amended it again in 2001 and added the most recent changes in the F.A.C.T. Act in 2004. Those amendments define some of the vague terms used in the original law. For the first time the FCRA has some teeth to it. The 30-day period has been locked in.

No information about your medical history, procedures or provider of medical services can be reported. Inquiries by cannot happen without disclosure to you in writing. Third parties (i.e. car dealer) are no longer "restricted" by the bureaus from showing you your report and more.

Continuing our discussion, let's dig deeper into section 611 and how to use it to your advantage. We'll begin with the term "inaccurate". Although inaccurate could mean almost anything, we interpret it to mean any information showing on your report, which, has been noted incorrectly in any way. Such as wrong dates, account numbers, balances, or prior paying history.

In other words, if any single piece of information, even if it's just a part of a larger piece, is being reported in an inaccurate way you have a legal right to dispute the account, and the credit bureau must delete it within 30-days from receipt of your letter.

However, simply calling the bureaus attention to the fact that something is listed wrong will not get it removed. In fact doing so will only make it easier for them. They will simply correct the dollar amount or date and leave it there so this idea in and of itself is not the way to go other than to give you the legal justification you need to file your dispute.

The second requirement of section 611 refers to information "that can no longer be verified". This is probably the most common reason why information is deleted from a credit report. Even if they can find the account, they usually can't verify it as required by law. Depending of course on which law you base your request.

Remember, the burden of proof is on the bureau. This requirement is why some credit repair companies and books tell you to hit them with dispute letters over and over. My thoughts; **luck and B.S. will only take you so far**. You need strategy not luck in this endeavor.

Generally, non-verifiable information is information which for whatever reason is no longer easily accessible to the creditor. Meaning they no longer maintain the physical records necessary to justify or prove a debt. Remember, it's not enough to simply claim a person owes a debt, they must prove it legally.

Non-verifiable could also mean the debt was reported incorrectly right from the beginning or altered along the way and is now impossible to verify because whatever records exist don't add up to what was reported. Either way it must be deleted.

As previously stated the new law states the bureaus have 30 days from the date of receipt of a consumer's dispute letter to investigate and respond to the consumer. Keep in mind **this is the weakest way to remove information** because today they have fax, email and other means of speeding up the process.

Section 611 also says if the "completeness" or "accuracy" of any item of information is "disputed" by the consumer, and that dispute is directly conveyed to the consumer reporting agency...etc.

The most common credit question people ask is, "how could it be possible to remove an account from a credit report when you really owed the money?" The answer is right here, by saying "completeness" or "accuracy". The law gives you the right to dispute information based solely on those grounds and does not make it a requirement we either admit or deny owing a debt to begin with.

Remember in this country we are innocent until proven guilty. A credit report is an indictment, which is defined as a written accusation. It either accuses you of being good or bad at paying your bills. Regardless, all accusations must be proven before they can stand.

Victims of crime, insurance companies stalling on payments for medical care or other benefits, Illness, Injury, job loss, natural disasters, war, recession and other mitigating circumstances should be taken into consideration but aren't when considering one's credit standing.

Congress didn't add sections to the law to provide relief or assistance for those who fall victim to any of the preceding unforeseeable circumstances. For creditors; it's easier to report the negatives to the credit bureau rather than make the effort to report it correctly upfront.

Just remember when someone you think knows about credit tells you you can't dispute if you "really" owed the debt, the law says you have the right based on the completeness or accuracy and if any one element of a debt is incorrect you have a legal right to challenge it.

The second section of the FCRA providing a legal way to remove information is section 605. It defines the length of time (statute of limitations) any piece of adverse information may remain on your report. Section 605 says a Bankruptcy can remain for 10 years and any other adverse piece of information for 7 years.

This is where the infamous seven-year period came from; but seven years from when? The law says in the case of bankruptcy, it's 10 years from the "date of entry of the order for relief" or the "date of adjudication" as the case may be.

For other adverse information it is 7 years from the "date charged off to profit and loss" or the "date of entry". The law says the reporting period begins at the end of the 180-day period, which begins at the commencement of original delinquency or date charged to profit and loss whichever the case may be. So six months after the account is closed for example.

There are other sections in the law that are important to pay attention to. For instance, **section 604**, which **defines under what circumstances a credit bureau, can give out information** about you.

Once again the law contains another vague phrase, "_legitimate business need_." In other words the credit bureau can sell your credit report to any company who can present a "legitimate business need" which could literally mean anything!

It could be to an insurance company who wants to sell you life insurance, an auto sales company who wants to sell you a car, a credit card company or anyone else who thinks they have a good reason like a collection company all without your knowledge or permission in many cases.

This particular section of the law is without question the most dangerous to an uneducated consumer because it gives any business the ability to not only pull your credit report virtually at will, but to report information about you with no obligation to establish its validity first to the credit bureau. I say "uneducated" meaning with regard to your rights under the FCRA.

A company or individual can report a collection account, judgment, bankruptcy, or other adverse information by mere virtue of the fact they are a "subscriber" or "member" of the credit bureau.

Meaning if they are a credit bureau client they have an application (online web site) to use when reporting information. No one at the credit bureaus checks this information when it's reported because there is no requirement to do so in the law.

The law says the bureaus need to establish *"reasonable procedures to ensure maximum possible accuracy"*. For their part the bureaus have disclaimers on the web site used by creditors and collectors when reporting. Where the entity reporting the information must assure the bureaus the information they are reporting is in fact accurate. Guess what? It rarely is.

Later in the Back Door chapter we'll discuss how to put the creditor or collection company in a position where they are forced to prove it or remove it from your file. For now remember that unless you pull your reports and challenge negative information it will stay for a minimum of seven years accurate or not.

The amended FCRA states you can notify a bureau you wish to have your name and address removed from any mailing lists they sell forever. I strongly recommend that you do this.

To become a "Subscriber" or "member" of the credit bureau, all you have to do for the most part is request to be one. When a company becomes a subscriber they receive a package from the bureau with all of the instructions and software and or access to online application they need to both pull and report information.

In that package is a disclaimer (*indemnification*) from the credit bureau stating the bureau in no way guarantees the accuracy of any item of information contained in any consumer file, and they completely rely on the companies who do the reporting to validate any accounts or claims.

They pull a credit report on the individuals who are the principals of the company asking to be a subscriber to determine "character". Now I'll bet that makes you feel a whole lot better doesn't it?

A credit bureau is considered by the courts to be nothing more than a conduit of information. Therefore they are not responsible for the validity of any piece of information appearing on your report until and unless you dispute it. In other words, they don't ask their subscribers for any actual proof when an account is initially reported.

Section 606 defines under what circumstances a business or other entity may request information about you. In this section there is another vague phrase, "_Permissible Purposes for Reports_". What does that mean? It means as long as the bureau can say the company requesting had a "permissible purpose" or "legitimate business need" they can sell the report to them. This section is additionally important because too many inquiries on your credit report scare off potential creditors.

The reason for that is they may think you are bouncing around trying to get credit and they are also curious as to why you were denied by the other lenders. You know, "what do the other companies who denied this person know that we don't".

Of course they rarely take into account it might have been you who said no and kept shopping for a better deal. On mortgages and cars most creditors will assume when seeing multiple inquiries you were shopping rates. Oddly on other items like credit cards they don't seem to view it the same way. It is important to keep inquiries to a minimum to avoid this perception.

The flip side of section 606 is that it gives any company the right to put anything on your credit report without telling you and without having to prove it first. This is without question the most dangerous and frustrating of the process and system. The idea someone can put anything on your report without your knowledge or consent or even having to prove it first is definitely a pitfall congress did not foresee.

Yes in theory a collection agency must send you a letter stating you allegedly owe a debt and that you have 30 days to dispute it or they will proceed with collection efforts however many agencies don't send the letter for that reason. If you dispute it they must prove and in most cases they can't. So they call you again and again vs. sending a letter.

This is the reason the credit bureaus have little or no liability. If it's left to the discretion of a company or individual to report information and the accuracy therein, then the credit bureaus themselves can only be seen as a conduit for that information. What did the Reagan administration call it? Plausible deniability right? The credit bureaus being a "conduit" of information is the same way tabloid magazines get away with some of the stories they print. All they need is someone to swear it's true and they can print it.

The same rule applies to a credit bureau. As long as the creditor or collection agency is doing the reporting the credit bureaus are off the hook because they're just reporting what they were told and the law does not require proof of the claim unless you request it. **Note to self**, request it!

As mentioned earlier there is another clause in the law called "reasonable procedures to ensure maximum possible accuracy" but it is so vague it's virtually useless unless you know how to put the credit bureau in a position of liability.

Nevertheless the law is helpful in removing negative information from your report because it leaves the door wide open for what type of information can and should be removed and then provides a time frame for it to be done if you know how to enforce it.

The principle problem with this section of the law is that it doesn't lay out any specific guidelines for the credit bureaus to follow when they're investigating a consumer dispute. This means **they are left to their own devices in deciding how best to verify information**. They could try to verify by making a simple phone call, sending an email or notification through their online application or by mailing a form letter to the creditor and relying on the creditor to respond.

Of course this means the credit bureau must rely on the individual who answers the phone, responds to the letter or email to be thorough in verifying the information. This presents a major problem because so many of us have similar names and although we think everything is based on our social security number it's not. So it often happens that accounts on your report which are not yours get verified as if they are.

Additionally the collector / creditor is in business to collect the money. Therefore they are not validating the dispute in an unbiased way. As long as they "certify" to the bureau the information is accurate the bureau will accept their response. What does "certify" mean in this case? Unfortunately this is not clearly defined but boils down to "we swear it's true".

File Duplication happens because when the credit bureaus call a creditor to verify an account they tell the person who answers the phone the exact name, address, and social security number of the person who is disputing the item.

The problem is if your name is similar to that of the person who really owes a debt, the collector or person in the credit department of the company who is being contacted now just looks for the first person who owes them money with the same or similar name and assumes it's you.

In other words the credit bureau hands you to them on a silver platter and then relies on their thoroughness and honesty to verify it is in fact the exact person who owes the debt and not someone with a similar name or address.

Well if you're in the collection business you assume everybody owes a debt and they are all liars. So when a credit bureau requests for them to verify and they find someone with a similar name in their system, there is an automatic assumption it must be you or the person they are being asked to validate for in computer disguise and they're *gonna get cha* and teach you a lesson.

So if your name is John Smith and the credit bureau calls to verify for a Jonathan E. Smith, the collector verifies the debt as belonging to you regardless. Are you angry yet? You should be!

The amended law still leaves many things out or provides weak assistance at best and should be resolved in a future amended version. A good example would be to add a section with respect to what should happen when you pay off a debt.

Currently there is no incentive in the law to pay off an old debt. Nothing in the law says that when you do pay them off, the account will be deleted or upgraded to a positive one.

The lack of such a section is the reason I advocate getting your credit report cleared up first and negotiating the debts later when it will truly be a win, win situation for both you and the creditor. When you owe you have no leverage to negotiate unless you have put the creditor or collection agency in a position where negotiation is the only way they'll get paid. We'll discuss this in later chapters as well.

Another example of a needed addition to the law would be adding protections for those who are victims of natural disaster, serious medical issues, violent crime and other issues not controlled by the consumer but devastating to one's financial life.

Here's the question, should those who are victims of circumstances well beyond their control be punished as if they simply ran up the bills and didn't pay? My answer to this would be "no". What good does it do to punish someone who's house was destroyed in a natural disaster or who has a life threatening illness or worse still, is a member of our military who put their life on the line for their country and returned home wounded and broke? That negative philosophy serves no one.

Until new amendments to the law are passed, we are forced to rely on the current one, so read this book carefully; it will serve you well both now and in the future. If you want to help facilitate the passing of the new law you can by writing to the

House Subcommittee on Financial Services.

Their address 2129 Rayburn HOB, Washington DC, 20515. Their phone number is 202-225-7502, give them a call and tell them you want the law amended to…

1) Protect consumers hit by
    a. Natural Disasters
    b. Violent Crime
    c. Serious Medical Issues
    d. Returning Vets or the families of soldiers lost
    e. Innocent Spouse (Divorce cases)

2) Dismissed or withdrawn bankruptcy not being reported.

3) Restoration of credit upon repayment of debts

4) Removal of negative info from one bureau auto removed from the other two.

You would do yourself and every other American a great service. Remember, congress is for the most part a reactionary body. If we don't push for change it will not happen. Unless of course they are affected personally then they move quick and decisive.

You could also post your thoughts about these issues on our Facebook page and we will be happy to pass it along to those fine folks in Washington. Our Facebook page can be found at (http://www.facebook.com/creditwarfare). We hope to hear from you soon.

CREDIT REPAIR PROCESS – Fundamental Strategy

Aright, now you've received a copy of your credit reports from all three major bureaus and it's time to go to work. The first thing you'll notice is they're all different. The reason they are different is because each company that extended credit to you in the past gets their information from the bureau of their choice so they may not, and often do not, report to all three. Here's where the fun begins.

The other thing you'll notice is in cases where they do report to more than one bureau a given account may appear differently on each credit report. Why? Because each company has its own method of reporting information and then humans get involved. For instance, they may report to one bureau in May and the other in July. Obviously they can't both be accurate.

The account was charged off on a certain day, but they reported it when they got around to it. In other words, you stopped paying in April, and they didn't report it until March of the following year perhaps. It happens all the time and the bureau will hold the information for seven years from the date the account was closed or the date of *last activity* which we'll get to later.

You may notice there are accounts you don't recognize. The bureau calls these "Overlapped" or "Merged" files. Your file gets confused with someone else's file. The sad part is this happens all the time and when the consumer complains to the bureau they get told to prove the accounts are not theirs.

Now that would be a neat trick; to prove something *isn't* yours. Not to worry, the burden of proof is not yours to carry. Make sure as you go through the reports you make a note next to every inaccuracy.

Remember, the law says anything "inaccurate" which means just that, "beyond the statute of limitations", or "non-verifiable" must be deleted. How do you know what is and is not inaccurate? Any old bills or notices will help you determine when the account was closed and how much was owed at that time.

If you don't have an old bill lying around you'll have to go by your best recollection. One thing for sure, the amounts and dates on the old bills won't match up with what's showing on the credit report. Every detail counts! It's not your job to prove anything but it helps when dealing with the moral issue of removing information for accounts you feel are really owed and had to know for the sake of your conscience were reported wrong.

Ok, a few more points to keep in mind at the beginning of the process. First, *do not* use the form supplied by the credit bureau for disputes. Why? Because they offer you multiple choice options as for why you are disputing the information most of which lead to the information staying on your credit report. They offer choices like paid, satisfied, settled, etc. all of which mean the information stays.

Stay away from the form unless you are monumentally confident you can control yourself and not choose a check box for convenience sake that essentially admits you owed but perhaps less money or at a different time. Remember, you don't need to reveal anything to the bureau. They have to prove the information contained in your report is accurate, verifiable and within the statute of limitations.

Always dispute every negative item the first time. The reason being that the law says the bureau has the right to deny your request for reinvestigation if your dispute is "_Frivolous or Irrelevant_". If you try to dispute one thing at a time by the second or third time they could claim your dispute is Frivolous on the basis you didn't dispute everything initially. In other words, they'll think your just trying to see what you can get away with piece by piece and consider the dispute invalid.

Ok, so where do you begin? How do you decide the best way to construct your dispute letter to get the best initial results? What on your credit report will establish a legal reason for dispute? I know what you're thinking, "finally the moment of truth". Now we get to find out how credit repair companies who advertise in the paper and online do this and charge hundreds or thousands of dollars for something you could and should easily do for yourself so let's get to it.

As with any problem, we first lay out the plan for solving it, so **we'll begin with a short outline** as follows:

A. Obtain a copy of your credit report from all three major bureaus. [If married get reports for both spouses separately]

B. Decode each account so you're aware of its status.

C. Analyze and record any discrepancies or inaccuracies. [Dates, amounts, account #s, etc.]

D. Review all other information [name, address, ss#, former address, inquiries, public records, etc.]

E. Design your dispute letter to cover all of the accounts you want deleted, Remember leave nothing to chance! [Include all items]

F. Send your dispute by certified mail return receipt requested or paste it online in their dispute form text box and keep the confirmation email they send thereafter. This establishes proof of mailing or receipt. [You can send certified to a P.O. Box]

G. Wait 30 - 40 days for your corrected reports to come from the bureau and follow up accordingly. [Every time you dispute the bureaus will send corrected reports to you for free showing what was removed and what wasn't removed]

CREDIT REPAIR – Detailed Plan of Attack

1) If you are sending your dispute via regular mail you may want to consider handwriting it. Believe it or not, the bureaus get thousands of requests a day. Some from attorneys, some from credit repair companies, and the rest from regular people. The lawyer letters go straight to the legal department. The letters appearing to be from a credit repair company get sent back because the bureau is under no legal obligation to respond to them. The letters appearing to be from regular people get handled first.

2) Mention all of the items in question up front. As stated earlier if you try to do it in pieces the bureau will probably respond by saying your argument is "frivolous and irrelevant".

3) If sending a paper letter always send your letter certified mail, return receipt requested or make sure you keep the dispute confirmation email. If you don't, there will be no evidence you ever did. P.S., you can send certified mail to a P.O. BOX. You can also send overnight mail if you use the U.S. postal service.

4) Only dispute the items which are inaccurate, non-verifiable, or beyond the statute of limitations. Don't worry; in 25 years I have yet to see one completely accurate credit report.

These rules are important because the credit bureaus will reject any letter that in their opinion appears to have been sent by a credit repair company. Your letter should be brief and to the point. Keep in mind, your objective is to improve your credit situation, not to find a sympathetic ear.

Sample letters can be found in the back of this book to help you get started. Just one last time I will remind you to send certified mail return receipt requested or archive the confirmation email they send if you are confident enough to use their online form. Be diligent and the results will come.

This is a process ladies and gentlemen, your credit problems did not occur in one day nor will they go away in one day. However, after the first attempt you will see some results and then it will be a question of time and which strategy is best for following up.

When you dispute for the first time you may be nervous about taking the first step because it's a step you've never taken before. You may feel unsure approaching the credit bureaus for the first time. Relax; there is no need to be anxious at this point because you still don't know which creditor, collector or bureau is and isn't going to put up a fight.

You see, after you dispute the first time the credit bureau will re-investigate the accounts in your letter and about five weeks later they will mail or email you a corrected report showing which accounts have been deleted, updated and which companies allegedly confirmed the information.

This is where the real fun begins. At this point you will know who is going to fight and who isn't. Meaning that until you see which companies claim they validated the debt and which ones didn't you haven't really started the process. It's round two and beyond that requires more knowledge and strategy.

Most books of this type tell you to barrage the bureaus with letters of dispute until eventually the negative items fall off but if you do as instructed here using the law you won't have to worry about reinsertion or any other issues moving forward.

So where do you begin the process? Very simple, you list of the accounts being reported negatively in one general letter. You can choose from the first three letters contained in this book to get the ball rolling. Simply choose which ever letter comes closest to your situation. If your accounts are old, use the letter for beyond the statute of limitations.

If they were paid off or are being listed incorrectly use the letter for inaccurate information. If the accounts listed are completely unfamiliar to you, use the letter for information which does not belong.

If your debts were incurred by a former spouse there is a sample letter for that as well. You can combine these into one letter if necessary. This may seem overly simplistic to you now but the only thing you want to accomplish at this point is to get the ball rolling. It is important to understand how to trigger their system in order to get them to remove the damaging accounts. To do this you need to pull one of three triggers.

The first is for "inaccurate" information. Just saying the accounts are inaccurate is not enough; you must provide a reason why. In other words, you need to give a reason they will accept as to why the information is inaccurate. However, never give a specific reason like saying the dates are wrong, the dollar amounts are wrong, or the accounts were paid off after the companies closed them. You can honestly generalize and avoid being too specific.

Remember, paying the debt off does not provide legal grounds for having an account removed from your report. Have I confused you? It wasn't intentional. The point is if you give them specific information they will just update your file with whatever information you gave.

The fact the dates, dollar amounts, account numbers, or names are listed incorrectly does give you the right to dispute, but are not grounds in and of themselves for the bureau to remove the information.

Still confused? Ok, here's an example. If you're accused of owing money to a company or individual and they report to the credit bureau stating you owe $2000.00 when in fact you owed $1000.00, you have legal grounds to dispute with the credit bureau.

When you dispute, they have an obligation under the law to re-investigate and attempt to verify that the account is either being reported correctly or incorrectly... So you would use the letter for information which is being reported inaccurately and say you never owed "two thousand" dollars. You are not obligated to tell them you did owe one thousand. The law clearly states it is the responsibility of the credit bureaus to maintain "reasonable procedures to ensure maximum possible accuracy".

When a debt is reported with the wrong dollar amount or date or any other incorrect information it violates two federal laws because the Debt Collection Practices Act states that "information which is false or should be known to be false" cannot be reported to any third party.

We are often the victims of this problem in the form of being denied loans because a debt looks to have happened more recently or for more money than was truly owed. Though it is not our obligation to supply the credit bureaus with the intricate details of our financial lives, it is our obligation to see to it that our rights are not violated because of laziness or arrogance on the part of collection agents, creditors and credit bureaus.

Most importantly, if you do give them specific information, you will have given the credit bureau the information they needed to hold on to the negative account permanently without having to request validation from the creditor or collection agency. So it's partially a game of semantics in the beginning. You use words like "paid", "promptly", "in full". But you don't say when, in what manner, and how much.

If you're arguing about dates for late payments you don't say it was late in April instead of June. You merely say it was never late in the month of June and leave it up to the bureau the process to deal with determining accuracy.

Remember, it's their job to find proof of whatever they are reporting, not your job to hand over information they aren't entitled to. Now take a deep breath, fifteen minutes of your life, and get the process started.

Now you've written your dispute letters. Make sure you look them over carefully before mailing them or submitting the online form. Remember, leave nothing to chance right? (Sun Tzu the Art of War: "He who is prepared and arrives on the field of battle first will be victorious"). You mailed them certified mail return receipt requested or archived the confirmation email they sent once you submitted the form online right? So far so good.

Now the clock is officially ticking. The bureau now contacts each disputed account's source and requests certification of the information as it was reported. 30 days goes by and you receive updated reports from the bureaus. When you review them some information may be deleted or updated and other info may have remained.

First you'll want to check and see if the reports are consistent. In other words, if an account was deleted from Equifax was the same account removed from Trans Union? If not someone must be lying right? They can't both be telling the truth in terms of "validating" the debt if there were two different outcomes. Don't let your emotions get the best of you here when you see some of the accounts remained the first time out. Keep telling yourself "It's a process" not a magic wand.

If you call the bureau(s) to argue about the accounts they didn't remove they will try to trip you up. How you ask? Well they might say something to get you riled up like "all of the accounts have been confirmed" which will lead you to believe your efforts failed. They do this to get you to either go away or start arguing with them. When most people start arguing they get upset and don't think clearly leading to mistakes in the conversation the credit bureau can use to impeach your initial letter. Stay off the phone with the bureaus and creditors for now.

Every change or deletion to your credit report is a major victory for you because every time a credit bureau removes anything from your credit report they are admitting there were in fact incorrect pieces of information on your report.

This is extremely important to remember because once something, anything, is deleted from your credit report the bureau has lost its ability to claim "frivolous and irrelevant". By deleting or updating any information, they have in fact admitted to incorrect information being on your report to begin with. You may not realize it at this point but there is recourse for you on several levels should you need it later.

Note the differences between accounts in relation to the corresponding collection accounts and between your three credit reports carefully, the differences lead to other clues of what really happened during the investigation. For instance, let's say your report had a Visa account being reported as "charged off" by the original bank and reported again as a collection account. Now your new credit report comes and the original account as reported by the bank is deleted. This tells you the original bank could not or did not verify the information and therefore the bureau removed the account from the report. However, they left the collection account regarding the same Visa card and list it as having been confirmed by the source. Not bloody likely!

How on earth could they have legitimately confirmed the account through the collection agency when the original creditor failed to confirm? I know what you're thinking. The original creditor gave the information to the collection agency when they assigned them the account. Wrong! Collection agencies only receive permission and basic information when they receive a new account. It comes in the form of a contract stating the name, address, telephone number, account number, and balance of the debtor, that's you. It does not come with the original contract, statements etc... And therefore the collector must rely on the creditor to "validate" the debt.

When the collection agency receives a dispute from the credit bureau generated by you, they're supposed to contact guess who? The original creditor. Ain't that something? So why then would the original creditor fail to confirm but the collection agency does? Could it be the collection agency earns their living collecting debts and if they don't collect they don't make money? Clearly the information was not verified between the creditor and collector.

Maybe it's the fact that many collection agencies actually buy the debt from the original creditor and if they don't collect they actually lose money. Possibly, it's that there are few if any collection agencies that know or even care there are laws regarding the collection of a debt.

Most likely it is because the collector did not do what the law requires in contacting the actual creditor and requesting the necessary documents to validate the debt. They simply replied without hesitation (or actual knowledge) to the bureaus stating the debt is "validated" "certified to be accurate".

Regardless, once the original creditor fails to comply the game is over legally. Oh there is one other small violation I failed to mention. Let's use the same scenario and remind you the original creditor did not or could not respond.

Maybe the reason for that is the account was originally charged off more than seven years ago and the original creditor knows it can no longer legally be reported. They also know they have already collected some of the money by selling the debt to a collection agency. If they validate beyond the seven year window they violate the law. So they are no longer interested in the account. A collection agency cannot keep information on your credit report the original creditor failed to verify or was proved to be inaccurate.

They also can't report or cause to be reported any information which was originally reported by the original creditor for any time period beyond that of the original statute of limitations. This means when an original creditor reports on your account as closed or charged off, the first reporting action begins the seven year statute of limitations. We know this because the law says seven years from the date the account is placed for collection or charged to profit and loss as the case may be.

If a collection agency reports an account to a credit bureau after the original creditor closes or charges off the account, they are in fact trying to extend the seven year period in order to continue to punish you until you pay them.

The credit bureau considers the reporting of a collection account as a "new account". Talk about double jeopardy! Even the FTC's own manual (Federal Register – 40 years of experience with the FCRA) which is supposed to be used as the guideline for credit reporting says a collection account does not extend the seven year period.

Where you ask? In the **Federal Register** under the **section interpreting section 605(a) (4) listed as #3 on page 57** of the document it states "The term placed for collection means internal collection activity by the creditor, as well as placement with an outside collector.

Placement for collection occurs when dunning notices or other collection efforts are initiated. The reporting period is not extended by assignment to another entity for further collection, or by a partial or full payment of the account".

Now, it would be fair to say almost all collection accounts are the result of a previous default on some type of revolving account, charge card, or contractual agreement. If this is true, then the reporting of any collection account once the original account has been deleted is a violation of the statute.

What the government is saying here is if an account is removed from your credit report by the original creditor, because it was charged off more than seven years ago, or for any other reason, then no collection agency can continue to keep it on there after the deletion. **This one fact alone is worth more than its weight in gold.**

Additionally, if the original creditor cannot verify the validity of the account, then collection agencies do not have the right to continue reporting it either. Pay close attention to this information, this is the most efficient way of removing collection accounts, repossessions, foreclosures, and charge offs from your credit report. That's allot of credit improvement from one strategy!

Summary – If an original creditor's notation on your report of a negative account is deleted for any reason, the corresponding collection account (3rd party) cannot remain. In criminal law this is called "fruit of the poison tree". Additionally a collection agency cannot extend the seven year reporting period by placing the "collection" on your report as the seven year period is calculated from the date the original creditor started internal collection or sent to an external collection agency.

NOTE: Do NOT sign a "re-payment agreement" with a collection agent or original creditor. You can negotiate or "settle" a debt without creating a written agreement. If you want to do it in writing make sure there is language requiring the creditor to "delete" or "remove" the account from your report once you live up to your end of the deal. If not you gave them a legal reason to continue to report the negative account for an additional seven years by signing such an agreement.

CREDIT REPAIR – Round Two - Re-Investigation

When you receive your corrected report for the first time, it's quite common to see some of the information from the original report deleted. The remaining items in dispute will be marked "Verified" or "confirmed by source". Don't let this discourage you; it is just part of the game. The first time around the only method they use to verify a disputed account is an email or notification to each creditor.

The reason this is so important to understand is when you receive a corrected report and there are items listed as *"verified"*, you need to keep in mind the initial result you're seeing is based on the creditors, collectors and bureaus taking the path of least resistance. They emailed the creditor or collection agent requesting validation or confirmation of the account, got an electronic response in the form of a return email or through their online application and accepted it as the Gospel.

You see, the person at the other end simply entered some basic Information like name, address, account # etc., which by the way they were given by the credit bureau representative in the email and said the account was in fact yours. The credit bureau never considers that the creditor may have made a mistake. Why should they? They're only a conduit of information anyway. Of course if they wanted to be certain The information they sell was accurate they would require proof up front or at least upon verification.

The key point to remember here is it is not enough to prove you may have existed. The law says they must prove the account was being reported accurately. Simply knowing a person did business with a given company and at some point in time and may have had a balance is nothing in the way of proof.

So how do you handle your second attack on the bureau to get more results than the first time? There are several ways depending on how hard you want to push.

Let's back up a bit and take a look at the flow of one's credit life or more importantly the "ebb and flow" of it. You get credit by "applying" for it. You use it and if you don't pay on time you lose it. This is when collection efforts begin.

First the original creditor starts calling and mailing you to resolve the outstanding debt. If you don't respond to them for a while they will eventually send the account out to an external collection agency. The collection agency either buys the account at a discount or receives it on consignment meaning the account is theirs and when they collect on it they keep a percentage and send the rest to the original creditor.

If you follow my advice and dispute the debt in writing sent certified mail return receipt requested to the collection company they must;

1) Contact the original creditor and obtain proof of the debt.
2) If they do not obtain proof of the debt they must "cease collection of the debt".

It is extremely important for you to remember that if you do dispute a debt as mentioned here and they don't provide the proof, the debt doesn't exist. If the debt doesn't exist they can't collect on it or report it to the bureaus.

So now fast forward to where we were with the prospect of re-disputing the remaining items. If upon your re-investigation request you let the bureau know you had requested proof of the debts in the past directly with the Collection Company and or creditor and they didn't comply you have put them (bureaus) in a position where they must remove the negative accounts.

This is by definition the "Back Door" strategy discussed in detail later. They receive your original dispute, allegedly investigate and send you a new report showing some items remain not knowing you were prepared in advance for this likelihood by having requested validation on your own long before. Let's talk strategy for a moment shall we?

The second time around you're dealing with the fact the credit bureau thinks it has done its job and verified the accounts you have disputed. They don't want to do any more investigating because it costs them money and employee time. So the real question is, how do you get the bureau not only to re-investigate your continuing claim but to remove more if not all of the remaining items in dispute?

By having requested validation on your own directly with the creditors and or collection agencies via certified mail return receipt requested you have irrefutable proof they are either unable or unwilling to validate the debt.

Pay attention here. When you dispute your credit report the process the bureau uses to confirm the debts belong or that they should be removed is as simple as an email or web notification. The other side needs only to return fire stating yay or nay. No actual proof is required by the creditor / collector at this point.

That you requested proof prior to this event directly with the creditors / collection companies as described here and did not receive said proof is all the muscle you need to force the credit bureau to remove / delete the negative accounts from your credit reports.

Think of it this way. The bureau trusts the other party to tell the truth when it asks for confirmation of reported negative accounts.

They accept the electronic response on faith but once you confront all parties with return receipts and copies of the dispute letters sent to the creditors there is no way out for the bureau or collector / creditor.

The bureau is faced with the reality that (a) the creditor or collector didn't actually validate the debt and (b) the creditor / collector is faced with the certainty that if they continue to report it at this point they'll be in violation of two federal laws. It's Check Mate!

SUPERVISOR ASSISTANCE – Taking it Up A Notch

When you are in round two and approach as just explained on the previous page you need someone other than a first level customer service rep who has the authority to help get the remaining issues resolved in accordance with the law. The advantage to this is a supervisor has the ability on their own to remove the accounts if they feel it is warranted.

Additionally, a supervisor knows a little more about the law than the first level person you deal with before being transferred to a supervisor and can be persuaded to follow it if of course you lay out the case for them. When dealing with a supervisor remain calm and in control at all times. They will not let you yell at them. They may even try to get you to make mistakes somehow by giving them information verbally you did not intend to give and was not in your dispute letter.

Simply stick to what you wrote in your letter and have it in front of you when you are speaking to them. Try always to talk to them on a personal level. For instance, tell them because of this problem you cannot get the mortgage you wanted or the job you deserve. Don't be afraid to ask how they feel about that personally. You'd be surprised at the answer you might get. They're human too! Yeah I said it. Some of them (just a few) are actually from this planet, look like the rest of us and on occasion have a conscience.

Bottom line, when you speak to a supervisor regarding your re-investigation you want to let them know you have those letters and return receipts from disputing with the creditors. Make them understand the creditor may have electronically validated the debt to them but was unable or unwilling to do so in writing to you.

It is important to point out that the 30 day window for the creditor or Collection Company to validate passed and therefore under the FDCPA 809(b) the debt no longer or ever existed. Therefore it cannot be reported on any credit report.

LEGAL DEPARTMENT – Establishing Leverage

If all else fails you may want to consider sending your dispute to the bureaus legal department. Does that scare you? Nonsense! A lawyer's job is to keep their client out of litigation whenever possible or practical. When you deal with a company's legal department you are dealing with individuals who understand whether or not you are in the right legally speaking and more importantly whether or not their client is vulnerable. In many cases this could be a major advantage and save tons of time for you.

For instance, there may be things on your report that truly do not belong to you, or maybe there are accounts which are long beyond the statute of limitations. In either case, the legal department will be much more likely to have those accounts removed than anyone else because they know how much trouble it could mean for their client if they don't and you decide to file suit.

Additionally, you may want to write to the legal department if you used the "Back Door" strategy and the companies did not comply and the customer service rep at the bureau doesn't want to cooperate either. Only the legal department of the credit bureau will understand it could become a potential problem for their client if the information stays.

When you deal with lawyers you need to remember they could care less about your tales of woe unless you can demonstrate that based on their clients negligence you are or did experience a major loss or hardship. So when you write to them get right to the point first then tell them what these problems have done to you personally. Be very specific about the events that took place and let them know which section of the law you feel you were violated under.

Remember, they know the law, so be certain you have complied with whatever section you are basing your complaint on or whatever section you feel their client [the credit bureau] did not comply with or blatantly violated.

It is OK to tell them that unless they help resolve the problem you will seek legal assistance and pursue any and all remedies provided under the law. You want to let them know you are not going to go away quietly and will not tolerate being brushed off. Lastly, it may become necessary to have an attorney contact them on your behalf.

Keep in mind if you have to go to the expense of getting an attorney and you are in the right, the law entitles you to attorney's fees in addition to everything else. If you follow this book, you will always be in the right.

If the bureau says they won't honor your request because they, in their infinite wisdom, think you are using a credit repair company or third party, call them and get a supervisor on the phone and say the following, "Can you please show me where in the law it says I can't seek assistance or advice from someone other than you".

They will respond with "We (the omnipotent) are only obligated to investigate a claim which comes directly from the consumer". Ok so I got a bit sarcastic here but trust me this happens from time to time.

This brilliant rebuttal is based on section 611 of the FCRA. It says and I quote, " If the completeness or accuracy of any item of information contained in his file is disputed by a consumer, and such dispute is "directly" conveyed to the consumer reporting agency by the consumer" etc., etc.

You need only remind them of section 610(d) which says "The consumer shall be permitted to be accompanied by one other person of his choosing, who shall furnish reasonable identification" etc., etc. In other words, you have the right to have your grandmother represent you or advise you whether the credit bureau likes it or not.

FRIVOLOUS AND IRRELEVANT

The old "frivolous and irrelevant" trick. As Maxwell Smart used to say "99, I've got this one covered". This term cited in the law (section 611(3)) is left open for many interpretations but the bottom line is the bureau has to be able to prove your entire dispute is bogus.

Obviously without the benefit of being clairvoyant or doing the investigation, they couldn't possibly know that. One reason they may claim or try to claim frivolous and irrelevant would be "a failure by a consumer to provide sufficient information to investigate the disputed information" as stated in 611(3a).

If this happens to you don't panic. A letter or email stating they have not or will not do the investigation because they believe your claim to be frivolous and irrelevant is not a tough one to overcome. You simply adjust the dispute to be a bit more directed. As an example you could simply re-write it stating you never owed $1,000 to that company vs. stating I never owed Xyz Company in a generic way.

I can't impress upon you enough how important persistence is when going through this process. These companies have hundreds of employees being paid by the hour. They are expected to complete a certain number of investigations per day. They are not going to give any one person's request special attention unless they feel there is a reason to.

THE BACK DOOR – Powerful Credit Repair Tactics

We touched on the back door strategy a bit earlier. Now I want to delve deeper because not only does it give you the best chance to have information removed from your credit report but it also sets the stage for protecting yourself against lawsuits by those same creditors and collection companies.

As I pointed out in the "Round Two" chapter, once you have disputed through the bureaus, they may maintain some of the information was confirmed by the source. There are some very important questions to be asked here.

1. Who exactly is the source?
2. How exactly did they verify it?
3. Was it in compliance with the law?
4. Which law?
5. Can they prove it to you?

Let's start with who the source is. The source is whoever is currently reporting the account to the bureaus. There is a distinct advantage to dealing with a collector as opposed to the original creditor. Because the law says they must prove the debt to you in writing, they're forced to contact the original creditor.

This means they don't possess the necessary information in house to prove the debt. The original creditor is usually not willing or not able to compile the data and send it to the collector in time for them to make copies and send it to you in accordance with 809(b) FDCPA

The second question was, "how did they verify it?" Because they don't have the correct documentation at their disposal, they're forced to validate the debt electronically almost always without ever even attempting to contact the original creditor and verify the information first. No court in the country would accept this as sufficient proof of a debt.

The answer to the third question, was it in compliance with the law? Depends on which law we rely. If the dispute was done through the credit bureau, then we are talking about the FCRA which only says "reasonable procedures to ensure maximum possible accuracy." If we are talking about the FDCPA (Fair Debt Collection Practices Act), it becomes a whole different matter. This of course, answers the fourth question as well.

As for the fifth question, "can they prove it?" This is where the fun begins. The collection companies hate being made reminded there is a law they must comply with and if they don't, not only do they not get to collect the money, but they could actually be open for a lawsuit which they would lose.

In other words, in this case the best defense is an aggressive offense. By putting them on the defensive, you accomplish a few things. The phone calls at home and work stop right away. The pressure you have been under for some time is released, and the collection agent is now in a very uncomfortable position.

You may ask, why do we not use this tactic in the beginning of the process? The answer is that at first we want to test the water so to speak and see what will be removed with minimal effort.

Sort of like throwing all of your credit problems into one big sieve and seeing what falls and what stays. Also we don't want to alert the enemy to the fact that we're going to and are capable of attacking unless it becomes absolutely necessary.

Remember, the shortest distance between two points is a straight line right? Why should you have to go through the headache of dealing with collection agencies, when you can have the credit bureau do it for you? This almost always leaves the collection agent in a no win situation. Now it's just a question of exactly how to use this to your advantage. So without further adieu, let's lay it out.

Under the FDCPA (Fair Debt Collections Practices Act) you have the right to dispute a debt and require proof of it from whoever is attempting to collect it (section 809(b)). The law says until the collector obtains proof of the debt in writing and forwards a copy of it to you; they must "Cease collection of the debt". The same section also says they have a total window of 30 days to complete this task. Sounds pretty cut and dry to me.

Now pay close attention to this because it represents the best way under the law to deal with the collection agency and the credit bureau at the same time. We'll begin by setting the scene. You have disputed directly to the credit bureau and now there are a few accounts left on your report the bureau has noted as "confirmed by source". They then tell you they have completed their obligation and now you'll have to take it up with the creditors themselves. If you did not have a copy of this book here is where you and everyone who claims to be credit repair clinic get stuck. Most importantly, at this point you feel defeated because the credit bureau has said it's basically over.

Fear not! You're the one who is in complete control. By sending one simple letter (#11 Back of book), You will put the collector in a position where by they can't collect on the debt, can't call to harass you or move forward with any action against you successfully and put the credit bureau in a position where they must remove the item.

Lastly you'll setup a layer of protection against any future lawsuit from an attorney they try and send or sell the debt to. Why? Because by using this letter you have formally requested in accordance with the FDCPA 809(b) that the collector verify the debt (allegation) in writing within 30 days and "cease collection of the debt" during this time frame and forever more should they fail which they do most of the time. By virtue of their noncompliance another section of the FDCPA 807(8) comes into play.

The following conduct is a violation of section 807(8) "Communicating or threatening to communicate to any person credit information which is known or should be known to be false, including the failure to communicate that a disputed debt is disputed".

If the debt collector fails to comply with your request under section 809(b) of the FDCPA, not only do they lose their right to collect the money, but they are also violating the law by allowing the information to remain on your credit report in a negative fashion. Obviously if they didn't validate the debt as required, the debt "is known or should be known to be false". If that's the case then it certainly cannot legally remain on your credit report can it?

At this point you send the credit bureaus copies of the letter you mailed to the collector requesting proof of the debt, and a copy of the certified return receipt, which of course you have because you followed my instructions right? You send those items to the credit bureau and simply request they remove the account on the grounds there has been no validation of the debt as required by law. You might also want to mention you suspect they (the creditor / collection agency) never actually confirmed it to begin with. Well, if they did, why wouldn't the collection agent confirm it to the alleged debtor if they were so willing to confirm it to the bureau?

Keep in mind the purpose of this chapter is to develop a strategy to force the credit bureaus into acting based on the only part of the FCRA that establishes liability for them. The "reasonable procedures to ensure maximum possible accuracy" clause in the law gives us the muscle so to speak to force them to remove information which is being reported in violation of the law. By demonstrating the original creditor or collection agency could not or did not verify the debt we prove our case and justify our demand that it should no longer appear on our report.

There are a few more rules to remember. Like everything else there are secrets to this game as well. They are important, so don't take them lightly.

1. Make sure, just like dealing with the bureau, you send these letters certified mail return receipt requested. **DON'T FORGET!**

2. From the moment you mail your request, don't contact the collector again or answer any calls.

3. Make copies of everything you send (don't moan, just do it!)

4. Request every possible piece of proof you can think of. (Original app, canceled checks, receipts, invoices, statements etc.)

5. Wait no more than 31 days from the day they receive your request to follow up with the credit bureau and request deletion of the account. Collection agents even more so than credit bureaus will deny ever receiving anything from you if you do not send it certified mail. They use scare tactics to get people to pay them. The last thing they want to do is actually work for the money.

Additionally, do not under any circumstance should you contact the collector by phone once you send your request. They may try to claim they verified it to both you and the bureau over the phone and you will have assisted them in buying time to attempt to get the necessary information to do just that.

When the 31st day comes, the game is over! Your next move is to send a letter to the credit bureau with a copy of the letters you sent to the collection agencies and request they delete those accounts from your file. From a legal point of view they must delete the accounts because the collector did not comply with the law, but they may try to stall, claiming they must hear from the collector directly.

Not so, the law says "reasonable procedures to ensure maximum possible accuracy". Once they "have knowledge" the account has not been validated as required by law, they must delete it. If they don't remove it they may become liable for damages which an attorney can assist you with.

Two more things to mention here that may help you. First, you have the right to file a formal dispute with the FTC in Washington. They have a division called "Credit Practices" and are equipped and ready to assist you in your effort. The other option is to contact the House Committee on Financial Services.

Remember, the FTC only takes on issues affecting many people at the same time. The sub-committee may choose to take on issues on an individual basis if they are valid. Here are the address and phone numbers to both.

FTC Credit Practices Division
60 Pennsylvania Avenue NW
Washington, DC 20580
202-326-2222

House Committee on Financial Services
2129 Rayburn HOB
Washington, DC 20515
202-225-7502

A few final points when contacting the government at either location. Send copies of your credit reports and letters sent to both bureau and collector along with proof of certified mailing. Include a cover letter explaining the mitigating circumstances surrounding the case. Give them the names of anyone you have dealt with at the bureaus or been abused by from collection agencies and their respective phone numbers.

Once again follow up is critical! Follow up with a phone call a few days after they receive your letter to see what advise they can give you or assistance they can provide.

Don't underestimate the power and influence of either of these agencies. They earn their living being the "white knight". Meaning they will help you if you have established a solid case and present it correctly.

There is an important lesson to be learned here, that is, most of us run and hide from collection agents when they call because we feel guilty about owing money. They use that guilt and fear to intimidate us into paying something nobody has proved is a valid debt, (valid in accordance with the law). This section teaches us that rather than run from them, we should fight.

By using this section to put them on the defensive, we eliminate the fear and guilt all in one shot, and nine times out of ten, they will fail to comply. Therefore, they must "cease collection of the debt" forever. So don't run and hide. Turn and fight! All bullies hate when the victim actually puts up a fight. They expect by using intimidation and fear, they will make you give in without giving them any trouble. Don't give them the satisfaction.

TWO POINT MATCH – Using Their Internal Process

So far we've discussed several ways based on the law to remove negative information from your credit report. All of them are solid legal ways to accomplish your goal. One of the other rules of war is to gather intelligence from the enemy camp. "Foreknowledge must be obtained from men who know the enemy's situation" *Sun Tzu*. This part is my job.

Over the years we have come across many internal policies of the credit bureaus but none as significant as the "Two Point Match". Remember, the FCRA does not say what exactly constitutes "reasonable procedures to ensure maximum possible accuracy". Over the years they have offered interpretations which imply a credit bureau should make more than casual contact (phone calls / emails) in their effort to verify consumer disputes. The FCRA requires the credit bureaus to send you a letter or email within five days of receipt of your dispute letter informing you of the exact process they intend to take to confirm the information. FCRA (611;2a)

The two point match concept is, you don't attack the enemy, you attack the enemy's strategy. Meaning there's no need to get into a verbal confrontation with the credit bureaus representatives when you already know how their decision making process works and what each person can do.

Now before explaining the "Two Point Match" strategy in detail, we first have to clarify some old myths about how the credit bureaus computers identify and separate our files from each other. Most of you probably think our social security numbers are the only piece of information needed to separate our files and that makes plenty of sense right?

We all have different social security numbers so it would stand to reason this method would be the most logical. I mean, even the oldest home computer could separate files ad infinitum with a unique seven digit number assigned to them.

However, the credit bureaus face a more complex challenge. They have designed their system so that all of your information factors in the computer's ability to know one of us from the other. Your name, address, former address, city, state, zip code, and date of birth all factor in to identifying us. The reason for this is there are many people with the same names (John Smith for example).

The bureaus know and have admitted to maintaining "merged / overlapped" files in their database. This admission is the reason they use more than just a social security number. If your social security number was the only piece of identifying information they used to prove an account was yours the system would remain extremely flawed beyond its current state of disarray.

So the current plan for solving this problem is the bureaus own internal policy on how to verify information. That plan is what I affectionately refer to as the "Two Point Match". **Is it killing you yet? Alright, here we go…**

In order for the credit bureaus to be certain an account is accurate, they need to contact the creditor and verify the account by confirming three key pieces of information. They are your name, address, and the account, case number, or social security number.

When the credit bureau contacts the creditor or collection agent to validate your dispute they ask them to verify these key pieces of information first to be sure the correct person is being reported on.

Then they worry about balances, dates, account numbers etc... Their primary concern is confirming the correct name, address and then the appropriate set of numbers (ss#, acct#, case#).

Now when dealing with someone's name they have a major problem. Women get married, people use nick names, change their name, use sir names, middle names, Junior and Senior of the same name and so on. Their next problem is to confirm your address. Talk about a problem! As you know, people on occasion move.

The only addresses the bureau has to go on are the ones listed on the credit report, and none of them have been proven. Last are the "numbers of choice" (ss#. case# acct#). The thing to remember about numbers is they're meaningless if the bureaus can't prove who they belong to.

Now, I want to remind you of something we haven't touched on enough, that is, "overlapping or merged" files. There are about 200 million adult Americans who are currently an active part of the credit system. The credit bureaus have bragged they have over 450 million files. Interesting isn't it?

They have more than two and one half times the amount of files then there are people. How could this be? Simple, Files get merged or overlapped all the time. Because their methods of separating us are so complicated, their computer system often gets confused due to similarities in first initial and last name in similar geographic areas and other nuances.

Lots of people are named junior or senior. Many people have common last names like Smith, Jones and Johnson etc. The system gets confused and creates new files for the same people or duplicates files from one person to another even though they are not one and the same.

Then there is the problem of creditors reporting to the bureaus and mistyping your name. That's right sometimes creditors and others who simply pull your credit accidentally type your name spelled incorrectly. Are you confused? Relax so are they.

In any event, they will try to confirm your name and address as the primary pieces of the puzzle. If there are any differences they will delete that account from your file and believe it was a merged account. So how does this apply to you? What exactly are the procedures to trigger the "Two Point Match"?

Most of us use our name differently at different times. For instance, you may sign checks one way, have your name on your driver's license another way and it may appear on other documents different from both of those. Any variation in the way we sign or have our name printed on anything could somewhere along the line cause our file to be merged with that of another totally different person.

You must know what exact name your accounts are listed under with each creditor. There is the possibility some of them are under your name with one spelling, and others are different, frankly, the more confusion the better. Also check the exact spelling of your name along with the address or addresses showing on the report. You can compare how your name appears on bills previously received from each creditor to how it shows on your credit report.

Next check what's listed under "Additional Information" on your credit report. You'll usually see some of your former addresses and different spellings of your name and maybe even different versions of your social security number.

That's right, if a creditor checked your credit in the past and in so doing transposed a digit in your social security number but got the other identifying information correct the bureau may show that social security variation under "Additional Information".

There is always the chance something listed is not your actual address or name. In fact, the odds are excellent. Remember, innocent until proven guilty? This is why. People have lost their jobs, insurance, licenses, and finance opportunities because of merged or overlapped files which were caused by this flaw in the credit reporting system.

We'll start with the accounts that don't match the way your name is listed on top of the credit report. The idea here is they have to prove every account, collection, judgment, bankruptcy and tax lien, belongs to you specifically.

Let's start with credit card charge offs and loans. We know they are going to either call the original creditor and talk to the first person they get on the phone or send an email / web notification. When they make contact the bureau will provide the name, address and social security number of the item in dispute to the creditor or collection agency. The person at the creditor or agency is only going to check their computer to confirm the account #, name, and address. If the credit bureaus employee gets confirmation from the creditor or agency they will not take the account off your credit report.

Once again a 3000 year old strategy comes into play here. "All battles are won before they are fought" *Sun Tzu*. You must know what the creditor is going to find out before you give them the opportunity to validate. For the two point match to work you must know how the information appears on your account with the creditor before you actually dispute. This way you only dispute those not listed correctly.

Just remember whether you're dealing with the creditor, a collection agent, or the bureau, to always be firm and stick to finding out the information you need to know while not giving them information they will undoubtedly use to make your life miserable.

When you're sure of exactly how they have the account listed you can use the "Two Point Match" to get the accounts not matching up with your credit report deleted. It is totally up to you to decide how your name should be listed on your credit report and on any account you may have.

Keep in mind, if they were going to sue you in court they would have to first prove the account was yours to begin with. Now let's say the account is in the hands of a collection agent somewhere and the collection agent is one who keeps confirming the account as accurate even though the original creditor has deleted it from your report. No problem. Send a letter to the collection agent asking for some kind of an invoice to demonstrate how much you owe on the account.

When they send you the invoice it will have the name, address and account number with which they have it listed. I know what you're thinking; we would be giving our current address to the collection agent and they would just change the invoice to reflect the current address.

You can either have them fax it, email or send it to a P.O. Box. If you are at a new address and have forwarded your mail from the old one you can have them send to the one they have and the post office will forward to you at the new one. It is safer to have them fax or email it. The bottom line is to find out what information they have on you. Without it, you're walking blind without a cane.

If you're dealing with a judgment, tax lien, foreclosure or bankruptcy be doubly sure about the way your name is listed on the court documents in order to use this strategy to delete them from your credit report. This too, is simple stuff. Simply go to the court where the case is filed and give them the case number. They will look it up for you and give you a copy, (some courts charge for copies). You can also try and pull it off the internet if your state and or county posts judgments online. If you can access it online do so and pay attention to the way your name is showing and if they have an address listed.

This gets a bit technical because the individual or company who filed the case against you most often did not file in the same name as appears on your license and that's all that matters. For instance, suppose your name is Lawrence Michael Smith and the judgment says Michael or Mike. Guess what? You can succeed in getting it deleted from your report. Maybe your last name is Wacko (nothing personal), and the document says Waco or Wako. You guessed it, check mate. The same thing applies to account numbers, dates, amounts, and addresses. **Are you excited yet? You should be**. This one strategy alone could literally save your financial life.

When you have the information from either the collection agent or the court, the next step is even easier. You simply send a copy to the credit bureau along with a copy of your credit report showing the difference in the information. As unhappy as they will be to hear this, they will be acutely aware they have no choice but to delete it from your report.

Now remember "reasonable grounds to ensure maximum possible accuracy"? Here is where it becomes your best friend. The law says the credit bureau must try to ensure the information in its files is as accurate as possible.

The current rule of thumb is, once they have knowledge an account is being reported incorrectly they must delete it or they may be liable for damages (FACR sec; 616 & 617). "Knowledge" would be when a creditor tells them or sends them a letter informing them an account should be deleted, or if you send them the kind of proof we discussed earlier. Either way they would have no choice but to delete it and send you an updated copy of your credit report to prove it.

There are many mentions of how the credit bureaus conduct themselves internally in this book. Each one is meant to give you a better understanding of how the enemy operates and thinks. Pay close attention. The more you understand about how they run their business the better off you'll be in your effort to free yourself from the financial shackles currently binding you.

I added this section in the book because of a situation brought to my attention years ago. For the sake of argument will call him John Smith. John his father and brother were all in a business together and due to economic hard times the business didn't work out. The three of them filed bankruptcy as a corporation. They did this to protect what little personal assets they had left. Not only did the credit bureaus put the bankruptcies on their personal credit reports but worse still, they reported all three bankruptcies on all three family member's credit reports.

You see, John as I've called him, had a brother named Jim and his father's name was John also. So the credit bureaus merged the files together even though the three men had totally different social security numbers. Why you ask? Because of the matching system they use instead of just relying on the simplest and most accurate piece of information to separate files, our social security number.

Therefore the two point match strategy had to be added to combat the credit bureaus careless process of file separation resulting in merged, inaccurate and overlapping files.

Additionally, attorneys, and other creditors often pay little or no attention to the spelling of someone's name, correct social security number or address. This presents a major problem for those of you who have had erroneous information show up on your report and then went to the extent of trying to provide proof it wasn't yours by sending in a "release of lien" or judgment or some other document which clearly in your opinion showed the debt has been reported incorrectly and doesn't belong to you. The two point match section guarantees you will receive the proper result.

ONE AGAINST THE OTHER – Positive Domino Effect

Over the years many people have asked me if you can play one credit bureau against the other in order to speed up the process of clearing inaccuracies off your credit report. My previous answer was always to say "no". The credit bureaus never cooperated with each other in any way including sharing information. This was probably due to the fact they were in direct competition with each other.

Although the law doesn't provide for one bureau to notify the other when information is deleted, it does say that once they have knowledge of incorrect information being in a consumer's file they have a responsibility to delete it. The most recent amended FCRA makes no mention of the sharing of information between the three biggest credit bureaus.

Sources inside the bureaus have said if you can get one bureau to remove an account or other adverse piece of information from your report, and then send a copy of the amended report to the other two bureaus as justification for removal from their system, the odds are pretty good the 2nd or 3rd bureau will go along and remove it as well.

Of course there are some things to be careful about here too. First of all if they are willing to remove information because you send them a different bureaus updated report, then they almost certainly are willing to add information, negative or positive, as well.

It's the negative information spreading like cancer from one bureau to another that concerns me. So how should you use this potentially powerful strategy to complete an otherwise burdensome job? Simple common sense will do.

Obviously if Experian removes information from their files in your name but still maintains other negative information the other two major bureaus do not have, it would not be a good idea to send the corrected Experian report until it was completely cleared up.

For this the strategy is fairly simple. Clear up one credit report completely and keep copies of every update that particular credit bureau sends to you as evidence the negative accounts both existed and were deleted. When you're certain there is nothing on the good report that can hurt you, send a copy of the proofs of deletion to the other two bureaus and request they delete the accounts as well.

I know earlier I said you need to clear up all three at the same time and you still should. The idea here is one may get done quicker because the bureau complies faster than the other two or for some other reason. In this case what I'm saying in this section is to finish the one that is closest to being 100% done and then use that to motivate the other two.

Here again *Sun Tzu* reminds us that, "All battles are won before they are fought". With a reminder to be very careful, call the other two credit bureaus that still maintain the negative accounts and get a supervisor on the phone. Tell them one of the other bureaus has completely removed the accounts from their files and you would like to know if they will do the same upon receipt of proof from the first bureau.

Be sure to get the supervisor's name and rank among the troops. If you get their commitment over the phone, follow up and send them the "update" the first bureau sent showing only what was deleted and send this document to the other two as proof.

Make sure to follow up with a phone call and check they have received it and will stick to their word. Limit the discussion to the fact you disputed the accounts with the bureau named on the completed report and the basic reason why you stated to that bureau those accounts were listed in error. **Do not** allow yourself to be dragged into a discussion of whether or not you ever owed those creditors money. **Do not** try to use this strategy before you attempt to delete the accounts from each credit bureau using the other strategies discussed in this book.

First of all, if you have more than half a dozen pieces of adverse information on your reports and you only attempt to dispute with one bureau with the thought in mind you will use this strategy to clear the other two, you almost certainly will find yourself fighting with the other two credit bureaus.

Why? Because they may take the position you got lucky with the other credit bureau but "you won't be able to pull the wool over their eyes". Who needs wool when you have the law on your side?

Secondly you will extend the total time it takes to get your life back together by not paying attention to the other two bureaus. The goal here is the move all of your pieces on the board in the right order to establish a case legally for the accounts to be removed.

For you A.D.D. people who don't want to read this entire book I can only say this, take your time and read it anyway. It will change your life for the better. That should be enough motivation for you to slow down a tad and absorb the information.

NEGOTIATION – Effective Strategies for Success

I want to state up front; trying to negotiate old debts off your credit report can be challenging. This is unfortunate and often depressing to discover because most of us are led to believe that if we make good on the debt, we should have our financial lives restored. However, most creditors and collection agents will tell you they can't legally "remove" or "delete" an account from your report, but they can "update" or "notify" the credit bureau you paid off the debt. Nonsense!

There is a galactic difference between "delete" and "update". I know some of you feel there should be no issue with an account that at one time had a problem and which you later paid off, but to the creditors, collection agents and credit bureaus it is a huge deal.

They not only will keep it on your report after you have paid the debt off but will update the file as of the date of the payment or final payment in the event you paid it off in pieces and potentially keep it on the report for another seven years as a result. Does that make you angry? It should. Additionally your credit score does not improve once you pay off a charge off or collection account.

Yes you are being punished for doing the right thing. In fact, by paying them and allowing them to "update" your credit report **you have actually paid to punish yourself**. The bottom line is there is no provision in the law protecting or rewarding you for paying off collection accounts or other debt. There are no rules issued by the FTC stating the bureaus must "delete" or "remove" negative notations once the account is made whole again.

With all that said let's move on. If you are intent on going this route, then by all means do it right. Remember their only interest is the money and nothing else. They can truly be "A wolf in sheep's clothing". They will say anything to get the money, including misleading you into believing they will delete the account from your credit report by using words like "update" or show as "satisfied" etc...

The only productive way of doing this is to make sure you get it in writing. This is difficult but worth doing so your efforts are not in vein. Do not depend on them to construct the letter, do it yourself. There is a sample letter in this book to use as a guideline. Under no circumstance whatsoever, do you send any money unless they have signed the letter and mailed it back to you or faxed you a copy signed by someone in a position of authority. Even if they say, "Just send the money with the letter and we'll sign it" or anything to that affect, don't believe it!

This is an extremely tricky process for most people. You are dealing with sharks who could care less about your credit or your money except for the fact they want it. You must be completely unemotional when negotiating with them. They rely on their ability to get you upset, feeling depressed and guilty to force you to do what's in their best interest, not in yours.

Best advice here is to conduct the entire negotiation in writing. Stay off the phone if at all possible. Make sure they understand you have no incentive to pay the debt off without getting your financial life back in return. Use the words "delete" or "remove" as opposed to "update" "notify" "show as paid" and so on. Make sure the letter is designed by you and signed by them and when you get a creditor or collector to sign it and send it back to you make sure you re-read it to be certain no language was changed or altered.

A collection agency will delete a collection account from your report if the original creditor tells them to do it or they realize it's the only way they're going to get paid. Try and negotiate with the agency in writing first. Remember, stay off the phone and do this only after you have sent letter 11 and they didn't comply. Then you're negotiating from a position of strength. Lastly keep the signed letter promising the deletion of the negative account for at least 5 years after the event so if for some reason the information is re-inserted down the road you can get it removed in days vs. months.

LATE PAYMENTS – Remove Them in Short Order

So, your credit report isn't so bad huh? Sure you only have a few late payments that's all. No big deal? Surprise! It is a huge deal to a potential lender and can severely affect your credit score. Late payments make them think either you're lazy or you don't manage your money very well. In either case, it will almost guarantee a denial of credit on a mortgage, business loan, or unsecured credit card even if the late payments were the result of a traumatic circumstance, a fluke or never actually happened.

You've gotten your reports and the late payments you made three years ago are still there even though you brought them current a long time ago. Most people believe once they bring an account current the late notation is gone, dissolves away or is removed somehow. Late payments are a grey area of the FCRA because section 605 doesn't discuss them directly. So how can you get late payments off your report when you really paid late?

Well believe it or not, there are a few different ways to accomplish this and still maintain the account on your credit report showing as "pays on time". The first method is by using the "Debt Collection Practices Act". Like earlier in the back door chapter when we ask a collector or creditor for validation of a debt, here to you have the right to have it proven to you that the account was paid late as reported by both the bureau and the creditor.

The theory works like this. You send a letter to the bureau stating the account was never late in say June of X year. They contact the creditor and ask if it was or not. The creditor responds with "yes it was late".

Now listen very carefully because this gets a little tricky. Many people have sent in payments that were posted late because of a slow processing system or the payment center for the company moved. When they see the late payments appear on their credit reports they get upset and wonder how it could have happened.

[The following hypothetical is to demonstrate how you approach the removal of late payments when they occur due to mitigating circumstances that were either unfair, unforeseen or beyond your control.]

Two years ago you paid late twice, once in March and once in August. You mailed the March payment in on May 1st, and the August payment on October 1st. The credit report states you were late in May and October.

Why? Because they often report it as of the date they received that month's payment. You do not tell them you were late but it was in March and August instead of May and October. Although this may be true, it is not grounds by itself to remove the late payments. As we discussed earlier, they will simply update it. What you say is that it was never late in May or October. This may sound like a game of semantics but it's effective.

At this point the credit bureau must ask the creditor if the account was in fact late in May and October. The creditor will check and see a payment was received in those two months and either not respond to the bureau or tell them to delete it. In the event the creditor comes back and says it was in fact late in those two months you have the canceled checks to prove them wrong.

Remember, the creditor is not going to want to spend time and money trying to verify an old reporting of a late payment on a good account that is current now when they have a whole stack of people who haven't paid at all. If for some reason they do, you try first to send the copies of the canceled checks to the credit bureau. Keep in mind once they have knowledge of information being reported inaccurately they must delete it.

If all of this fails we simply switch to plan "B". We reverse gears and go after the creditor by using the "Back Door Theory" discussed earlier. This time we request the creditor send us everything relevant to verify the account was in fact paid late in the months they reported.

We ask for, canceled checks and original application from the entire account history. You have a right to see it so why not ask for it. This strategy is for when you know the information doesn't exist, is incomplete or inaccurate.

Assuming the creditor is willing to go this far, they will discover there were no late payments made in the months showing on your report. In most cases they will not even respond to you within the time allotted by section 809(b) of the FDCPA, Once again it's checkmate.

At this point you send a copy of your letter which was sent to the creditor requesting proof of the late payments to the credit bureau along with copies of the return receipts from the certified mailings. Now the bureau has "knowledge" the debts or late payments have not been validated as provided for by law and must remove them.

The third strategy is to call the creditor and talk to a supervisor. Explain you are trying to get a job or a mortgage and the late payments are stopping you from doing it. Tell them you would appreciate it if they would delete it from your report so you can get the job or mortgage you're after. **This is called "back dating" the account**. It is easy for the original creditor to accomplish but can be difficult to persuade them to do.

Many times they will say they can't or even that it is illegal for them to do this. That is simply not true. You just need the right person to get it done. Ask for the head supervisor or vice president of the company. These people usually have the power and ability to delete or back date information without anyone else's permission.

NOTE: Don't stay on the phone and argue with someone who is unwilling to help. Hang up and call back. Nine times out of ten you'll get someone else. Repeat as necessary.

This will work about 70% of the time if you are still a customer of theirs and have been current for some time (6 to 12 months). Tell them you are a customer for a long time if that's the case and as small a problem as it may seem to them, it is a mammoth size problem for you and your family.

Of course this particular strategy is based on people's personal decisions, but in most cases if you present it right they will usually oblige. Remember, they're human too. They have lives to live and families to care for just like you. Gently remind them of that and let them do the rest.

NOTE: Always date a payment (check) for the date the payment was actually due no matter when you send it. If it was due January 1st and now it's February 10th you date the check 1/1/year. Down the road you'll have a cancelled check for the correct date which may be useful in requesting your late payments to be removed. It also helps with keeping good records as to what check was for which actual payment.

THOSE PESKY INQUIRIES – Off They Go!

Every time you apply for something it generates an "inquiry" on your credit report to show you applied and what creditor pulled your report. It will show the date the inquiry happened and who pulled it.

It's incredible how everything has to be presented as something that works against you instead of for you, and every one of those things interpreted as being negative must be because you made a mistake or acted irresponsibly in some way. Too many inquiries in a short period of time can create the perception you are either desperate because you need the money or you are shopping around. Shopping around is not an issue.

The bottom line is, inquiries can and do lower your credit score and can even stop you from having the things you want and deserve. But like everything else, there are remedies to the problem. In fact there are several potential remedies you can add to your arsenal.

Number one is to find out which inquiries are what are called "prescreening or soft inquiries". A prescreening inquiry is one where a company pulled your report because they wanted to offer credit to you. It is made possible because of the, "legitimate business need" clause in the FCRA. A subscriber to the credit bureau pulls your credit because they might want to do business with you in the future but doesn't want to waste their money on advertising or extending an offer if you can't be financed.

Anyway, all three of the credit bureaus have a policy of removing prescreening inquiries without too much of a struggle. Allegedly, when a company uses the bureau for this purpose they must use a different subscriber code.

This code tells the bureau the inquiry was for the purpose of prescreening. The credit bureau may place these inquiries in a section of your report with a heading like "inquiries only you can see" or "inquiries creditors can see". Obviously, if you are going to dispute under this premise, you should check your credit report and note the inquiries that are repetitive or those you cannot remember giving permission for.

The second possible method for removing inquiries is to send your dispute to the decoding department of the credit bureau stating the inquiries in question were illegal and they violate the "Permissible Purposes" clause in the FCRA.

Each credit bureau has a department called the "Decoding Department". They are the credit bureaus own internal investigation department for discovering if a company either pulled or reported information illegally through their system. They govern themselves by the "Permissible Purposes" section of the law.

In the Fair Credit Reporting Act, section 604 says a consumer credit report can only be provided under the following conditions.

1. By virtue of a court order.
2. By the consumer's own authorization.
3. For credit transactions with the consumer.
4. Review of collection account.
5. For employment purposes.
6. For the underwriting of insurance.
7. Determination of eligibility for licensing.
8. Otherwise legitimate business need.

Any inquiry not fitting one or more of these criteria is illegal and subject to civil and sometimes criminal sanctions. For instance, pulling a credit report on a non-applicant spouse or ex-spouse, for the purpose of selling it on a mailing list, in order to "check someone out", like a neighbor or coworker and lastly, pulling a report for the sole purpose of "prescreening" alone if you requested on the bureaus web site to be kept off their marketing lists.

They are permitted to inquire as long as they pull a group of reports and intend to make a genuine offer of credit to each meaning the creditor who caused the inquiry pulls many reports to send out an offer to those fitting their marketing model.

The decoding department will either check with that company to find out what their intention was when pulling the reports or they will delete it if they are familiar with the company frequently pulling reports while looking for clients.

The last strategy is to write to the company themselves. Believe me if you contact a company that pulled your credit report 2,3,4,5+ times and tell them unless they remove those inquiries from your report you will file a formal complaint with the FTC in Washington D.C., they'll consider it in their interest to remove it.

You have the right to request from the company that inquired into your credit, a copy of the application you signed giving them authorization to pull your credit report. If somewhere in the past you did sign an application with them, the odds they still have it and are willing to find it, make a copy, and send it to you in 30 days or less are slim and none. They are much more likely to notify the bureau to remove it. If you never did apply for credit with them they will discover that and remove it for fear of a potential lawsuit.

JUDGMENTS – Multiple Strategies for Removal

So you had old debts, you couldn't pay; the creditor sent it to a lawyer to file a lawsuit against you. He or She did and you were served with a summons and complaint. You had between 20 – 30 days to file an answer with affirmative defenses. You didn't know how to properly file a response and you couldn't afford an attorney so you just didn't show up. The court issued a default judgment against you and the lawyer put the information on your credit report. Sound familiar?

This is not in any way an impossible situation credit wise. You just need to understand the different potential strategies for removing judgments. There are several different ways to attack this problem. Before we get to removing a judgment from your credit report I want to discuss trying to handle these situations before they become judgments. Preventive medicine is always the best strategy.

Before an attorney files a lawsuit they typically try several times to contact you by sending a demand letter. The letter tells you they represent your creditor (alleged creditor) and you owe money. They demand you pay the debt by a certain date or contact them to discuss a resolution which is a code word for payment plan of some type.

Remember, at this point the creditor already tried to collect by sending their own letters and maybe even sent the account to a collection agency who also tried. If at any point in this timeline you had sent a letter disputing the debt and requested for them not to call you at any location for any reason you would have saved yourself quite a bit of aggravation and the account wouldn't have made it to the attorney. **Sorry for the "I told you so"** but I don't want you to ever forget how important that strategy is.

The good news is you can still send your dispute letter to the attorney if no lawsuit has been filed yet. That's right, they must comply as well. If you send letter 11 to the attorney when they send you a demand letter the lawyer will be put in the same position as a collector. They will first need to contact their client and request the docs you mention in the letter. They will know the window to accomplish this task is 30 days from the date of receipt. If their client doesn't send what was requested or doesn't do it in time the game is over and they'll know it.

Here's a good what if. What if you did dispute it with the creditor or collection agency and they then send to the attorney who files suit right away anyway? You are served and must file an answer right? No problem at all. Firstly; there is case law (**Supreme Court**) to back up the fact that a disputed debt cannot be reduced to a judgment without first obtaining and providing the required verification. *Heintz et al v. Jenkins*, (No. 94-367; 1995 U.S. Lexis 2840), decided April 18, 1995

To address this particular challenge you simply attach to your answer a copy of the letter you sent to the creditor or collection agency along with a copy of the certified return receipt from when you sent your dispute letter asking the court to dismiss the case on the grounds your rights under 15 U.S.C.; 1692g ; 809(b) were violated. In all likelihood the court will set a date for a hearing. At the hearing plaintiff's counsel will be asked if they have "proof" of compliance in accordance with 15 U.S.C. 1692g; 809(b). They won't. Game Over!

Every state has what it calls "Rules of Civil Procedure". These are the rules of the game for civil suits. Some states even provide you with the sample forms you can file with the court and case history to back up your position.

You may have to do a little homework to obtain documents or an affidavit, but a monkey could do this with the proper instruction. **Remember;** if you don't file an "answer" to the suit a default judgment will be entered against you. Big mistake!

To summarize this discussion, you have the opportunity to protect yourself and stop any future action on three separate occasions with the creditor, collection agency and attorney in that order prior to being sued.

In the future don't be foolish enough to ignore these opportunities to put the fire out early in the game and end up having to work backwards from a default judgment that shouldn't have happened in the first place now that you have been educated as to how to deal with this scenario.

In most states you must file your answer within 20 – 30 days from the date you served with the suit. If you are going to file a motion to dismiss you probably need to file that either before the answer or at the same time. Check with a local attorney or your court clerk for procedural time lines and or advice. The court clerk cannot give you legal advice but they can point you towards any resources the county provides online or otherwise.

In the next few pages we will show you how to file your answer and what according to the rules of civil procedure would constitute grounds for an affirmative defense or if you defaulted already getting the judgment vacated. Remember, these are not complex legal moves, so just read on and remember this is a very effective way to remove judgments, foreclosures, and tax liens from your credit report.

As I am not an attorney licensed to practice I recommend you consult a civil attorney before doing any of the following if you intend to attempt to, defend yourself pro se, file an answer, motion to dismiss, motion in opposition to summary judgment or have a judgment vacated after the fact. Each state has similar procedures and rules but time lines and format may differ and the advice of competent legal counsel is money well spent. The key message is to fight along each step of the process.

The first thing you and or your attorney will need to decide is whether your situation falls under one of the legal grounds the court will be willing to hear. Remember, the court is not going to hear arguments based on "mitigating circumstances". Those are the reasons or situations that led up to your not being able to pay the debt.

In other words, the government could care less what happened to cause you not to pay. They don't want to hear you lost your job, got hurt or sick and had to use the money to pay the rent, or any other excuse for nonpayment. Just like the credit bureaus they will only respond to a legal reason. Additionally an explanatory approach is useless from a defense standpoint.

The first of the legal reasons to file a motion to vacate or for new hearing is fraud. If you can demonstrate a company filed a lawsuit fraudulently, the court will not only vacate the judgment but may, if you file a counter suit and win, award damages.

Some examples of a fraudulent lawsuit would be, a collection agency suing you for someone else's debt like a relative or business associate.

Filing suit even though they have knowledge the debt was not owed i.e.; post letter 11, knowingly lying to the court in their affidavit / petition as to material facts. Proving these would not be too difficult for your attorney to prove or disprove assuming you are in the right.

The second reason would be mistake. In a "mistake" situation, you or your attorney state the reasons you believe show the plaintiff had no causation for filing in the first place. For instance, there was no evidence provided in the plaintiff's petition to establish you as guarantor on the loan or credit card or the debt was paid prior to the filing of the lawsuit.

Mistake as a reason may also be applicable when the court clerk makes a mistake while entering the judgment, the initial filing was by mistake, or the judgment was filed even though the case was dismissed, withdrawn by the plaintiff, or settled prior to judgment.

A third reason would be "Newly discovered evidence". What you're saying to the court is you have evidence which would prove the debt wasn't owed to begin with and wasn't available at the time the case was originally heard. This could be in the form of recently found receipts, contracts, or proof the products or services alleged to have been delivered were in fact not delivered.

With respect to contracts you might use this when for instance the contract said 12 months and they billed you for 18. This would also apply when you can prove you terminated a contract as set forth in it. There is also the potential the contract was illegal, however you're really going to have to do some homework to demonstrate this which is why money spent on a civil attorney is a good investment.

Proving the products or services were not in fact delivered or were but not as laid out by the contract, requires you either have a sworn affidavit from a whiteness, make the claim the plaintiff never proved to the court that it delivered, or show that the goods or services were never received. Like contacting UPS, and asking if they delivered a package in your name from that company to your address and if not to give you a letter stating so.

Once you or your attorney files the motion to vacate or dismiss the court will either schedule a hearing, or in some cases if you present concrete evidence the judge could grant the motion without a hearing. One last point, if the judgment is vacated, legally it no longer exists. If it no longer exists it can't remain on your credit report. If you file for a new hearing and are successful the game is not over. You'll need to be prepared to defend you position at trial. Again, it would be a good idea to consult an attorney.

In order to get the vacated judgment off your credit report you can approach it in one of three ways. First and easiest would be to demand the other party notify the bureaus to remove any notation of a judgment against you. You can also request an order from the court as part of your motion to vacate, dismiss or for rehearing.

Lastly you can send a copy of the court order vacating the judgment to the credit bureau with a cover letter telling them to delete it. If you were smart about this and hired an attorney you can have them do this last part for you.

BANKRUPTCY – A Detailed Discussion

In 1898 our government decided that on occasion people get into financial binds due to situations they couldn't foresee coming or didn't plan for. As a result, the economy suffers because these people became subjects of lawsuits, collection efforts and black listing. In order to provide for protection from these unfortunate events happening and wiping us out congress created the bankruptcy act.

It was amended in 1938 (9 years into the great depression) to include expanded voluntary access to the bankruptcy process. It was further amended in 1978 (again in the middle of a tough recession) and again in 2005.

The 2005 version was designed during the greatest economic boom in U.S. history. Not surprisingly the purpose of the new version was to make bankruptcy more difficult and costly to file. Don't you just love how congress plans ahead? They make it easier when things are bad as if they'll never improve and harder when times are good as if they'll stay that way forever. True genius at work.

In 2005 (the year they amended it to make things harder and more costly) over 2 million Americans filed to beat the deadline and use the old rules from 1978. In 2011 despite the new law; 1,362,000 people filed for bankruptcy including famous people and more than 47,000 businesses, which is expected to be surpassed in 2012.

The whole idea was to give an individual the opportunity to rebound from a financial catastrophe and be protected from losing their home and other essentials. Obviously they felt this served the greater good in that it allowed for a person to use the law as a parachute out of a financial disaster.

Unfortunately, many of you are now or may have been in a financial squeeze in the recent past. Perhaps you've been trying to pay one creditor while holding others off. Sooner or later the pressure builds and you start using money earmarked for the essentials like rent, mortgage, food, phone, electric, transportation and medical care to pay off your credit cards or cellular phone.

Like the rest who are unaware they can stop the bill collectors themselves and negotiate the debt, many file bankruptcy in order to relieve the pressure. (Reminder – Letter 11 to the rescue) While it's true that filing and having your debts discharged in a bankruptcy will legally free you from the responsibility of having to pay the debts, it also destroys your financial life for the next 10 years. I liken it to the financial equivalent of a nuclear weapon. There's only one possible outcome.

Here's a simple test question to ask yourself in the event you are considering filing a bankruptcy. Do you own any property or have assets you need to protect from your creditors? If you don't own a home or have other assets to protect filing bankruptcy is nothing short of financial suicide.

Consult an attorney about whether or not filing is for you but know going in that most attorneys know very little about the credit system beyond their own personal experience. If you live in a state with a homestead exemption / protection your house may not be vulnerable regardless i.e.; Florida.

It's simply a matter of education, if everyone knew there were two other federal laws they could use to their advantage they would rarely consider filing a bankruptcy. The main reason attorneys recommend bankruptcy is that bankruptcy is what they're familiar with and a relatively easy action for an attorney to file.

They evaluate your debts, create a petition, fill out some forms and file them at the federal court house. I don't mean to over simplify the role or work but in essence that's how it goes. If attorneys were to advise under the other two laws which are mentioned in this book they could save their clients from the same fate in most cases without filing bankruptcy, charging less and help many more clients making up in volume what they lose in gross fees for bankruptcy representation.

For the lawyer, filing a bankruptcy is in many ways cookie cutter in nature and much of the work can be done by their legal secretaries. Using the other two laws would represent uncharted waters for most. So if you were the attorney which venue would you advise people to take? If you find yourself in this predicament, take heart. There is a cure and you have found it. However, it will take some time to eliminate the problem.

One of the most common questions asked is, if I really filed the bankruptcy, how could there be any way to remove it from my credit report? If I do, is it legal?

As we mentioned earlier, the credit bureaus are not divisions of the government. They are just a business like any other. In order to not only understand how this is done, but why it can be done legally, you must first understand the basic mechanics of credit reporting.

Credit reporting agencies like Experian, Equifax and Trans Union rarely seek out information on their own. They charge a fee to their corporate customers for the privilege of reporting information to them and receiving it as well. All court actions are reported by the parties who initially filed them in court, not the court itself.

The only possible exception might be Tax liens. They are usually reported by the IRS or the state tax agency that filed the lien. Regardless, the courts never report the information on their own.

Everyone wants to know how a bankruptcy can be removed once it appears on your credit report? The answer is that all information verification completely relies on the individual creditor's ability to validate their claims against you.

The guidelines require the information: (a) does not exceed the statute of limitations, (b) is being reported "accurately", (c) is verifiable. In the case of bankruptcy, we know the information was not reported by courts but by the individual companies included in it.

So who then does the burden of proof fall upon? Right again, the creditors themselves. It is the creditors who must prove not only did the debt exist but that it was and is being reported in accordance with the law.

By now, hopefully, you have discovered the secret to deleting bankruptcy from your credit report. Let's lay out the strategy in detail in order to avoid any mistakes. The first strategy is designed to combat the thoughtless reporting of bankruptcies based on the initial "filing" of it prior to even knowing if the debts were discharged or not.

In the case of a withdrawn or dismissed bankruptcy the strategy is quite different from one where an order for relief was entered. Don't get frustrated or give up on this issue. Depending on the way the bankruptcy was reported you can remove it and in many cases do so in short order.

BANKRUPTCY STRATEGY – Accounts First

"Forewarned is Forearmed" Right? In other words you don't call the enemy and tell them when, where, and how you will be attacking. Remember the bankruptcy was reported by the creditors not the government. If you dispute the bankruptcy upfront, you make it easy for the bureau to verify because all they need is for one of the creditors to come through and it stays for ten years. Yes it's 10 years not seven for bankruptcy.

Keep in mind when you filed your bankruptcy you included a list of creditors in your initial filing. If you dispute the bankruptcy upfront, all the credit bureau has to do is get one of those creditors to verify and "you're up crits sheek pithout a waddle."

So obviously we want to remove the accounts included in the bankruptcy before we attack the bankruptcy itself. The accounts included in it went dead long before you filed right? Of course right. Therefore two facts are certain.

First, a bankruptcy does exist and regardless of what your credit report says, those creditors can't collect money from you which obviously makes you less interesting to them. They have people who owe them money now who they are actively pursuing. Financially speaking, you're a lost cause.

Because the accounts went dead long before the bankruptcy was filed, those creditors have long since had you in their "dead files". What is a dead file you ask? Dead files are accounts they can't collect money on for one reason or another. They are usually stored away in a warehouse or put on a disk and stored away. In either case it would take a great deal of effort for someone to physically go and look up a dead file account.

In almost all cases it is no longer in the creditor's interest because there is no financial gain to be had. Therefore, most companies do not respond. Even if they did, it would be drastically different from the way it was reported to the credit bureau.

You see, if the account was charged off a long time ago, the companies have sent it to a collection agency or an attorney who in turn added interest and fees to the original amount. By doing so, they make the debt near impossible to verify because the original principle amount would be so different from the way the debt ended up after collection attempts. When the debt was discharged in bankruptcy, it was discharged at the inflated amount. Therefore, if any attempt is made to verify the debt after, the burden of proof becomes more difficult.

Considering the accounts included in the bankruptcy were charged off long before the bankruptcy was ever filed, the odds will be much greater in favor of removing the accounts first using the techniques discussed herein. Once we have removed those accounts from the report there is no place left for the bureau to verify the bankruptcy except the court itself. Why? Because when the credit bureau deletes information they completely purge it from their system forever making it impossible for them to use those accounts to verify the bankruptcy.

The reason for this is that once information is removed for a legal reason, the bureau "shall maintain reasonable procedures designed to prevent the reappearance in a consumer's file, and in consumer reports on the consumer, of information that is deleted pursuant to this paragraph" (FCRA 611; 5c).

Under the (FCRA 611:Bi) - information can be reinserted if "the person who furnishes the information certifies that the information is complete and accurate". This is not an issue if you used the back door strategy and already proved the creditor didn't validate the debt in accordance with the FDCPA 809(b) discussed earlier.

The end game here is to get the bankruptcy removed from your credit report. Once the accounts included in it are removed it will be easier to challenge the bankruptcy itself.

Can't they just call the court and ask for verification of the bankruptcy over the phone? Under most circumstances the credit bureau is forced to request the information by mail. Remember two things: the bureau is a business like any other and is primarily interested in the bottom line.

Therefore, they don't like to spend any money they do not deem absolutely necessary. All of this must be done in 30 days as described in the FCRA section 611. Secondly a federal bankruptcy court clerk isn't paid and doesn't have time to validate information for a credit bureau by phone all day not to mention a phone verification wouldn't do anyway. There are many "Smiths" in the U.S.

Remain patient when going through this process. If you call the bureau, they will definitely try to get you to discuss each individual account. They will try their hardest to get you to say something different from what you wrote in your dispute letter. Remember there are several ways of removing any accounts from your report so follow the process and try to keep your emotions in check throughout.

BANKRUPTCY – Filed, Dismissed or Withdrawn

There are three particular circumstances related to bankruptcy we need to discuss further. The first is the mere filing of one which is reported on your credit report as "filed". The second is a bankruptcy which was "dismissed" by the court. The third is a bankruptcy which was "withdrawn" by you or your attorney.

These situations are particularly troublesome because the law only discusses "date of entry of the order for relief", "date of adjudication" and "withdrawn". It does not discuss "dismissed" cases as relates to the 10 year reporting period.

Like everything else there is a process by which a bankruptcy is conducted. Step number one is to file your case. Meaning you list all the creditors you are asking the court to discharge in bankruptcy. Then you file in federal court in your county.

To do that, you or your attorney must go to the court and file four copies. The bankruptcy court clerk gives you one of your copies back with the court's seal on it as a "true copy". Then you pay a fee and you're off and on your way having officially filed a bankruptcy. A notification you have filed is then sent to every creditor listed and they in turn notify the credit bureaus.

The bankruptcy filing gives you an "automatic stay" from any collection or civil litigation. If you're being sued it stops the lawsuit and the debt in that suit becomes part of the bankruptcy. This is the reason people do it. They are tired, frustrated, scared and hit a moment where they just want "it" (the stress of owing" over.

In many cases you could call this "surrender". You succumb to the pressure and tactics of the creditors and use bankruptcy to make it go away. Of course at this point most people rarely consider the consequences to their credit and ability to recover later but it does do the job which is why I refer to it as the financial equivalent of a nuclear weapon.

When the creditors notify the credit bureau you filed a bankruptcy the bureau notes your credit report with "bk filed, date, case#". This process is the only way the credit bureaus are aware a bankruptcy exists. The law states a bankruptcy remains on your credit report for 10 years from "date of entry of the order for relief" or "the date of adjudication". The date of entry is the date of filing and of course prior to any final disposition. The date of adjudication is the date the debts are discharged in bankruptcy. Either way the sentence is 10 years hence on your credit file.

It would be rare to find someone at any of the credit bureaus who knew and understood the law at all much less it's interpretations. This works to your advantage because if you remember to only deal with a supervisor when you call, it's not too difficult to get them to concede the law doesn't say anything about "dismissed" or "filed" bankruptcies.

The FCRA makes no mention of dismissed or filed bankruptcies. This is important because if you filed and didn't go through with it the case gets dismissed either voluntarily or involuntarily. If you filed through an attorney and change your mind the attorney can "withdraw" the petition. There is a difference as relates to your credit report between a bankruptcy that was withdrawn and one the court dismissed.

If you are in the bankruptcy process right now and decide you don't want to go through with it (i.e.; back door) ask the attorney to get it dismissed as opposed to being withdrawn.

Explain to them that from a credit standpoint you have better odds of getting any notation of it removed from your credit reports if it says "dismissed" vs. withdrawn. Reference FCRA 611:(d)(1) which states "If any case arising or filed under title 11 United States Code is withdrawn by the consumer before a final judgment, the consumer reporting agency shall include a in the report that such case or filing was withdrawn upon receipt of documentation certifying such withdrawal".

Do not ask the bureau representative to remove your bankruptcy in an argumentative way. They are not going to make the effort to check the law if you make an enemy of them. Always keep in mind they are not lawyers and do not know how to interpret the law.

Tell them section 611 of the FCRA says bankruptcies remain for ten years from the date of adjudication (date of discharge) or the date of entry of the order for relief. Plant the seed in their mind that obviously a dismissed, withdrawn, or mere filing of one is not mentioned in the law and was not meant to be on a credit report.

This is a strong argument when dealing with a non-lawyer employee of the credit bureau. They are human and a layman like you. Certainly they wouldn't want to be punished for something that never happened if they were in your shoes.

Additionally, you may want to remind them that judgments, foreclosures, and tax liens are not reported when they are filed, only when they are adjudicated. So why would a bankruptcy be treated any different? After all, bankruptcy is a judgment is it not? The fact it was self-induced does not legally change the fact that if it was never adjudicated it didn't happen in the eyes of the law.

Persuasion is the key here. You are attempting to convince the credit bureaus representative what you are saying makes sense. They are trained to do whatever their policy says and only a supervisor can make a spot decision without it.

The objective of persuasion is to ask questions of the other person whether in person or in writing they can only answer positively to. By asking questions they can only give a positive answer to, you can keep the conversation focused on the relevant subject matter that will help you accomplish your objective in a non-threatening way. How you ask? Easy, let's take this current example for instance. If I were handling the conversation it would sound something like this.

ME: Mrs. Jones, you'd probably agree that having any mention of a bankruptcy on your credit report is extremely bad wouldn't you?

JONES: Sure.

ME: Obviously if I actually went through with a bankruptcy it wouldn't say dismissed on my credit report would it?

JONES: No I guess not.

ME: I noticed that judgments, tax liens, and other court actions are not noted if they were dismissed, or withdrawn correct?

JONES: Yes.

ME: I also noticed the law says bankruptcies stay from the date of adjudication, which made me feel much better considering mine never was adjudicated or discharged which is what you see on your side right?

JONES: That's true.

ME: Great! So when can I expect it to be removed from my credit report so I can have my life back. It's the worst and only thing negative on there.

Does this sound a little silly? Well it is probably one of most powerful ways to persuade someone regardless of the issue. Besides, it's only meant to be a guideline for how to conduct your conversation when calling the bureau.

The principle thing for you to remember here is to only ask questions that bring about a positive response and to avoid making statements vs. questions. Remember this phrase, "when you say it they tend to doubt it, when they say it, it's true!"

The objective here is to demonstrate to the credit bureau that an action which was never adjudicated; therefore never actually happened. Meaning if there was no ultimate determination in the case like the debts being discharged or losing a lawsuit, in the eyes of the government the case never happened or at minimum it did not happen in a fashion you should be punished for. Although the law also says "date of entry of order for relief" which is interpreted by lawyers and the courts as the date of filing, a reasonable person could assume it means "date of the entry of the order to relieve the debt" or date of discharge of the debt.

Remember, the words "dismissed" or "filed" are not in the law under section 611. Therefore a strong argument can be made for those bankruptcies which are dismissed or have just been "filed" to be deleted. Keep in mind credit bureau employees don't know how to interpret the law so persuading them is more than possible.

The government's position on this is, as usual, confused. They don't seem to think it correct for a dismissed bankruptcy to be on a credit report, but they also don't seem to think it matters all that much. Of course nothing could be further from the truth and we (Credit Warfare) are trying to persuade them to fix this issue in the law.

That fact the bureaus don't search court records is why even if you have a bankruptcy that was actually discharged in court, and you tell the credit bureau it was dismissed, in most cases they will just change it to dismissed and send you a corrected copy. Proving once again they don't really check.

They don't see a dismissed bankruptcy as anything to be concerned about so they give you what you want and change it without even checking. This behavior can be useful later on in the process.

Remember, one step at a time. Don't jump from one strategy to another. You should attack in a methodical manner one move at a time. It's like a chess game; each move brings you closer to victory. The wrong move at the wrong time could cause unexpected and unnecessary frustration and consequences. I've seen people remove bankruptcies from all three credit reports in less than six months. That could never have been accomplished if they did not follow the strategies in order. As my mother used to say, "One miracle at a time".

REPOSSESSION – How to Protect Your Car and Credit

So what do you do when you're late on your car payment or mortgage and they are going to foreclose or repossess? Well, if you didn't know what your rights were you would be in a very stressful position and would come out of it worse than when you started. However, you are more educated now so obviously that's not going to happen now is it?

Repossessions and Foreclosures are two of the most depressing events that could ever happen to a person. You know, waking up one day and your car is no longer in front of your house, or coming home from work to find a notice to vacate on your front door, Very depressing.

However, if you know how to enforce your rights you can come out better than ok and even protect your credit along the way. Before we begin with the different strategies for removing these types of problems from your credit report, I'll first explain the process of repossession and foreclosure.

Here is the general chronology of events that takes place leading up to a repossession or foreclosure. You have a car loan or mortgage for a certain period of time and something goes wrong in your financial life.

Suddenly you find yourself trying to decide whether to pay your credit cards, cellular phone, cable and other bills versus paying the car payment or mortgage. Don't laugh, people do pay the cellular phone before the car or house because the cellular phone company will turn off the service sooner than the other companies will repossess.

The embarrassment of someone calling and your cellular or home phone is disconnected is usually too much for the average person to bear. Anyway, the lender starts by sending you late notices and calling you to collect. At first they try a soft approach and ask you to call them to discuss your account.

You knew you couldn't pay so you avoided speaking to them to avoid the guilt and stress. Some more time went by and they started sending notices saying you are "seriously past due" and "must contact them now"! This made you avoid more because if you call, they'll want the money and you don't have it.

Now you have a problem. They go into recovery mode and begin the repossession process. This usually happens with a car at 60 days or so late. With a foreclosure proceedings usually start when you pass the 90 day mark.

If it's a car we're talking about, they send someone to take it in the middle of the night while you're sleeping. If it's a house they file for foreclosure in court and serve you with a civil complaint (lawsuit). Either way it's time to stop avoiding and start paying attention because the sooner you take action the better off you're going to be. **It is always to your advantage to confront financial problems head on and not hide from them**.

What action should you take? Later on in the chapter titled "Preventive Medicine" we'll give you several strategies for saving the car, boat or house. For now let's concentrate on what to do when they already foreclosed or repossessed your property.

Since car repossession is more common than foreclosure we'll begin with that. First let's clear up a couple of misconceptions. If you voluntarily give a car back, it is still considered repossession and is just as negative as one where the lender came and took the vehicle themselves. Second, when you voluntarily give a car back or it's taken and you actually have equity in the car it is still repossession and shows just as negatively as one where you're upside down in the loan.

If you're wondering why a voluntary repossession is just as bad I'll tell you. Regardless of how the car ended up back in the hands of the lender they see it as a loan gone bad. Even if the car was a mechanical nightmare or you were lied to in some way about mileage, year or some other point of sale information, the lender sees it as an extension of credit they had to revoke.

Under most state lemon laws you have some protections against this but again, if you don't know what they are they're useless.

Many people are under the impression that if they bring the car back themselves instead of waiting for the lender to come get it this process somehow will save your credit and protect you from having judgments and liens put against you, Wrong! They still see it as money lost and will take every legal measure to regain what they feel they were entitled to.

So let's get to it, how on earth can you remove a repossession from your credit report when they really came and took the car or in the case of foreclosure when you lost the house and were forced to move? Much of what you read throughout this book explains the basics of why it's possible but let me give you the exact reason for this particular case.

First of all let's understand the process of repossessing a car or boat; we'll get to foreclosures in a minute. When your car is repossessed there is a legal process the lender must follow in their effort to collect on the money they feel they are owed. That process basically works like this.

They come and get the car in the middle of the night while you're trying to sleep but unable to because you're too busy thinking about how to solve your financial problems. After your morning coronary, when you realize the car or boat is history you have a new problem, how to get around. While you're busy trying to figure out another means of transportation, they send you a "love letter" reminding you the car has been repossessed and you have a fiduciary responsibility to pay the balance.

You're thinking, "No kidding". They tell you the car will be auctioned off in 30 days and you have till then to cure the debt. The 30 days goes by and you get another letter telling you when and where the auction is supposed to take place.

Believe it or not, you could conceivably show up and bid on your own car and end up owning it for less than you would have originally paid through the loan. After the auction you receive another letter telling you the car was sold and you now owe the difference between what it was sold for and what the ending balance on the loan was when the repossession took place. Of course they try to help you out by adding on all kinds of ancillary charges like towing, storage, interest, penalty fees and some other goodies to cheer you up.

All of what I just told you is completely predicated on the fact the lender follows or even acknowledges the law. Whether they do or not is almost completely irrelevant as to whether or not you can get the repo off your credit report. Why? Thanks for asking.

Because as usual, in all the confusion from repossessing the car and then auctioning it off, they make a truck load of mistakes in reporting it to the credit bureaus. They almost always get a collection agent involved after the car has been auctioned off. At that point they don't want to be bothered with chasing you for the money because they already got theirs and the car is gone.

They earned interest from you while you were paying, plus the down payment, and the auction money. They sold the invoice from the bad debt to a collection agent whose been calling you at work every day to remind you of what a wonderful person they think you are.

That's right; they sell the whole debt to a collection agent who then chases you like a shark chasing a wounded fish. Why? Because the collection agent has no image to protect or stockholders to keep happy and can therefore do almost anything they want to get you to pay a debt the bank or lender has already collected on if not made a substantial profit from. Does this bother you?, good, it should bother you that in addition to taking the car, making the money anyway, destroying your credit, and leaving you land bound, they then give it to someone else to destroy your self-esteem, reputation, income, and serenity. Owing money is one thing, but it doesn't and shouldn't mean you are a free target for collectors to humiliate and harass.

The collector who by the way knows that when the time comes you do pay, and in their opinion sooner or later everybody does, they get to keep money you never actually owed because the debt itself was paid long ago, pushes as hard as they can so you give whatever money you have to them before paying the next creditor on your list. Most people don't know the details of this process and therefore fall prey to each level of it.

The news is not all bad however. **Pay close attention**, I don't want you to get confused and make a mistake. As we discussed, when they repossess your car or boat you owe a certain amount of money based on the balance of payments you had left. Later when they auction it off you owe less because they collected money from the auction. The formula goes like this, (A (auction) – B (balance) = TD (True Debt)).

When they report the repossession to the credit bureaus they report the entire amount of the debt including all of the afore mentioned items. For example, if you owed $10,000 at the time of the repo, they probably will report it as a debt somewhere in the neighborhood of $11,000 to $13,000.00 because of all the other charges they add on.

When they do this they have violated the law. How? When they (collection agents) add interest and fees (often not provided for in the original contract) to the debt before getting a judgment they have made a mistake. Only a judge can make that decision or the original creditor based on the signed contract. Of course in this case not only does the collector add interest and fees but they also forgot to subtract the sale amount from when they auctioned the car or boat off from the total debt.

This obviously makes the debt inaccurate. However, the last thing you should do is tell the credit bureau they are reporting the wrong amount. As we discussed earlier all they would do is change the report to reflect the amount you say is the correct one. It doesn't matter to them how much you owed, all they care about is that the fact it was a bad debt and now has been confirmed and you helped them do it. It is the creditors' responsibility to see to it the information which is known to be false or should be known to be false **is not reported** to a credit bureau.

The fact it is being listed inaccurately means you have a legal reason to dispute it. However, now you need a legal reason to delete it from your credit report. This is why the "Back Door" chapter is so important. Once you have established the debt cannot be proven, the credit bureau must remove the account from your credit report.

There are other important strategies which can be applied to this situation. First you want to get a good grip on all of the facts. For instance, were you a co-signer on the loan or the "guarantor"? Was the account covered by insurance in the event of default?

Was the car repossessed more than six years ago and approaching the seven year statute of limitations? Was the car less than a year old and in the shop for repair more than six times? (Lemon laws). If you were a "guarantor" on the loan, even though the common theory is you are equally responsible, with respect to credit you're not.
FCRA 603(k)(1)(A)(3) states "Because the FCRA adopts the definition of "adverse action" from the ECOA (Equal Credit Opportunity Act), only an "**applicant**" experiences "adverse action" in the context of a credit transaction. See 12 CFR § 202.2(c)(1). A co-applicant is an "applicant" but a "**guarantor**" is not. 12 CFR. § 202.2(e). Regulation B states **that only an "applicant" can experience "adverse action" in a credit context** and excludes a guarantor from its definition of "applicant." 12 CFR Part 202.2(c)(1) and (e). See comment 603(k)(1)(A)-3

The company who extended the loan or credit card would be forced to prove the loan was granted because you the co-signer were in fact a "co-applicant" not a "guarantor". The co-applicant can be held responsible both financially and from a credit standpoint. The "guarantor" cannot.

So clearly when you sign for someone (which you should avoid at all costs) make sure you sign as "guarantor". If there is a line on the application you are asked to sign make sure the text under that line says "guarantor" and get a copy of it.

There have been several State Supreme Court decisions stating only the "applicant" or "co-applicant", can be held responsible for the monthly payments. The reason for this is other than the preceding legal reference is that sometimes people get divorced, business partnerships breakup, children forget to tell Mom and Dad they didn't make the payment as they promised.

The same applies when two people get divorced and one does not live up to the decree as adjudicated by the court. If the responsible partner or spouse was the "applicant" and you were an "authorized user" on a credit card or "guarantor" on the loan you are good to go from a credit stand point.

This is a major problem. People get divorced and the court says each of them is responsible for certain debts. One of them doesn't do what they were supposed to do and the other ex-spouse gets financially destroyed as a result. It is the "applicant" who bears the financial burden. For example the IRS has a protection for scenarios like this called "Innocent Spouse". We'll cover that issue later in the next chapter on tax liens.

Maybe you were in a business partnership that for one reason or another didn't work out. You had bank accounts together, leases for property and equipment together etc... The partnership breaks up and you find out later your partner used your companies tax ID number to acquire credit cards and other extensions of credit without your permission or consent.

According to the old school of thinking regardless of whether or not you consented to these financial moves you have a responsibility to those creditors. Imagine for one moment if this held true, every time things didn't work out between two people or entities the other could destroy the former legally and leaving only one possible source for protection, a lawsuit.

Even if you won in court it would be a completely different thing getting it off your credit report. However if a partner did as described here using the company tax ID you cannot be touched personally from either a debt collection or credit reporting standpoint.

In the case of divorce or the breakup of a partnership, you use the basic argument that the debt simply does not belong to you. It isn't that hard of an argument to make when you weren't the co-applicant on the loan or account. If the debt was close to seven years ago or more but is reflecting as if it happened much more recently, you use the back door to obtain proof of the fact it was charged off seven years ago or to prove the debt wasn't your responsibility.

In the event the loan or credit card was backed up with insurance in case you couldn't pay for some reason, then you need the original loan papers or application showing you chose the insurance and therefore the debt should have been paid. Legally, you kept your end of the bargain.

If the vehicle or boat was a mechanical nightmare, you generally need to show it was in the shop about half a dozen times in the first year to be able to use most lemon laws. The good part about this problem is the state in which you live will go to bat for you.

If you send them documentation it was in the shop several times in one year (the first year), they will contact the dealer or manufacturer and force them to not only take the vehicle back but to refund your money and not damage your credit report. For a copy of any lemon law or forms to file for relief, go online to your county court clerk or state statutes web site and do a search for it. It's that easy!

Remember, the primary mistake creditors make when reporting repossession is to report it with the total amount showing before the sale at auction on your credit report. This negligence on their part gives you the right to not only have it removed but makes them potentially liable for violating the "Debt Collection Practices Act" section 807 relating to information which is false or should be known to be false.

FORECLOSURE – Defend, Modify or Exit & Remove It

Regarding Foreclosure; the process is much longer and more complicated. The basic flow of events goes like this. You miss three payments (90 days past due). The bank shows the loan as "in default". They send to an attorney to foreclose on the property. You get served with a lawsuit for foreclosure.

You must file an "answer" to the suit within 20 – 30 days depending on what state you live in. If you don't file an answer the foreclosure will be granted by default and you'll be notified of a "sale date". You must vacate the property at some point (pre-determined) prior to the sale date.

Needless to say foreclosure is an extremely stressful process and quite costly for the bank. Before we proceed I want to give you a few **helpful pointers** so if you are in this situation you can do something to keep it out of foreclosure or get the mortgage "re-instated" by the bank. This may help you avoid a long nasty painful process ending with your leaving the house with a huge debt trailing behind you.

FYI – To you this process is new and represents the unknown which is what drives your stress and emotion. Use what you learn here. Be patient, persistent and polite. In the end the correct solution will present itself. Be ready for anything mentally.

1) Mortgages rarely go into foreclosure or default until they are 90 days or more past due. If possible pay the principle and interest portion of your payment (1 payment) inside the first 90 days keeping the account in a 60 day window vs. 90.

Get the bank to apply the P&I payment to the 1st month past due. You may need to push a bit but they'll do it. This keeps you in a 60 day window and away from foreclosure.

2) If you are 90 days past due or about to be and you cannot make a payment you need to act quickly to keep it out of foreclosure and get the loan into a modification team's hands. Most banks will not proceed with foreclosure while the modification process is going on.

   The federal government has clamped down on banks that did. There was a 250 Billion Dollar settlement in March of this year (2012) for this type of bank misbehavior.

3) If your loan is past 90 days and you have not yet been served and you are not in the modification process you can be certain your loan is on its way to an attorney to file suit. Call your bank and find out who the attorney is. Get the contact info for the firm. Most attorneys prefer to settle these issues rather than prosecute them (civil not criminal). You may be able to arrange a stipulation or late in the game modification agreement to get your loan re-instated.

4) If your mortgage is with **Bank of America** and you are getting nowhere with customer service regarding your request for modification you can reach out to the Office of the President. They will intercede to help get the loan into the modification process. While they don't do the modification in their unit they do have significant influence over the home retention teams and foreclosure staff. This helps expedite the process of stopping foreclosure.

To reach them call 704-386-5687. Ask for help from someone at the O.O.P. You will be transferred to a rep who "acts on behalf of Brian Moynihan" CEO of B of A. They can help you regardless of what you were previously told by other representatives.

5) **Short Sale** – Doesn't sound so good but can be a great way to exit the house and maintain your dignity. Your lender agrees to sell the house for less than you owe (assuming the house value has dropped below outstanding loan amount). You get out with no foreclosure on your credit report and no debt following you afterwards. If you know your income will not recover fast enough to make the payments presented by a modification this may be the best solution. There are lots of houses in the world. **Don't let your emotions guide this decision** even if your kids learned to walk there.

6) **Persistence** – when dealing with your mortgage lender regarding a modification try and remember to be both patient and persistent. The home retention reps have huge case loads. While they understand your home is everything to you and you are very concerned, they can't remember everything you tell them and get back to you each time you call.

   This reminds me; go easy on them unless they really botch things up. Always use honey before you reach for the vinegar. They catch hell from many people each day. You're more likely to make progress if they remember you're the nice one. Nice but persistence and keep copious notes about every conversation you have with them dated with the rep name and extension number.

7) **Deed in Lieu of Foreclosure** – As described in the Hud.gov web site "A Deed in Lieu of foreclosure (DIL) is a disposition option in which a mortgagor voluntarily deeds collateral property in exchange for a release from all obligations under the mortgage. A DIL of foreclosure may not be accepted from mortgagors who can financially make their mortgage payments". You basically surrender the house to them and they agree not to "foreclose".

8) **Modification** – First of all let me state up front you don't need anyone to help you get your mortgage modified. The only difference in what they might do is they'll be persistent and are familiar with the game. You can do this yourself and save thousands of dollars. Most of the larger lenders will help you modify your loan. They will need some documents to evaluate your income and expenses. There are some key numbers to remember before sending them anything.

   a. 31% - This is the dollar amount or percentage of your gross income the mortgage payment needs to use up. The range is between 31% - 55%.
   b. $729,750.00 – This is the max amount your loan balance can be to qualify.
   c. 40% - 50% - Debt to income ratio needed.
   d. 6 to 12 – Months it takes on average to complete the process.

There are several government programs to help you through this issue but remember to be honest with yourself. If you know you can make the modified payment then fight for it. If not you should consider either a short sale or deed in lieu as an exit strategy.

Here is the link to the government's site with resources for foreclosure.

http://www.usa.gov/Citizen/Topics/Family/Homeowners/Foreclosure.shtml

My thoughts; Take care of your family by keeping it out of the stress of foreclosure and all that goes with it.

TAX LIENS (FEDERAL OR STATE) – Remove Regardless

Having a tax lien on your credit report may seem like the equivalent of being called a witch in the puritan days. You are hunted by the IRS, banished by the lending establishment, and thought of as an all-around bad person by everyone else who of course live perfectly flawless lives.

As I'm sure you know, the IRS never makes a mistake and puts a lien on someone who really didn't owe the money or for the wrong amount right? Of course right.

In many cases they make the credit bureaus look like angels. They can destroy your life with little chance of being held accountable for their actions. They can put you in jail for Pete's sake, over a debt! Who said there are no debtor's prisons in the United States?

Do you think I'm being too dramatic? Well if you spoke to as many people as I have regarding this issue you'd be angry too. Here's my theory as to why the IRS, in addition to everything else they can do to you, decided to go after your credit as well.

In 1989 the IRS and Rudy Giuliani prosecuted Leona Helmsley (Hotel magnate and owner of the Empire State Building) for tax evasion, back taxes and mail fraud. Not a good day for Leona as she got 19 months in jail. Regardless this case set off a firestorm of reaction from all corners of the U.S. Helmsley broker the law and was punished for it however the message it sent to the rest of the country did not come across quite the way the IRS hoped.

Obviously you're dealing with a government agency with seemingly limitless power, which learned a lesson from the Helmsley case. They went too far. They made themselves look like the evil empire out to destroy anyone who dares to question their authority.

It turned out to be the wrong move at the wrong time. Not the act of prosecuting her; but making it so public and nasty. Though she clearly got what she deserved it terrified the tax paying public.

Many books came out telling of how to legally not pay income taxes or how to legally beat the system like the rich supposedly do. For the record, they don't. People started to sue the IRS publicly for intrusions of privacy and wrongful prosecution. A rebellious attitude took over the country and people learned of ways to not only negotiate with the IRS, but to negotiate or fight and win.

With all of this happening the government decided it needed to back off of its threatening posture a bit and look for new ways to punish and collect but not get the bad press the comes with prosecuting the average guy for back taxes. They of course still prosecute cases but typically keep the criminal division focused on those who cheat for larger dollar amounts and other malicious fraud and schemes.

The negative perception of prosecuting the "regular guy" caused them to discover the credit bureaus as a resource. They had used them before in certain cases but never realized the power of being able to destroy your credit. It's cheap, and accomplishes a whole lot more damage for a longer period of time and no one ever protests about it.

So they put a tax lien on your credit report knowing sooner or later you'll need credit and it will get in your way. Then you'll pay the lien in the hope that paying the tax lien will cure your credit problem only to find out later not only does paying not cure it, it prolongs the total amount of time the tax lien stays on the report. If there is a legitimate dispute or after the fact a release from lien you should be able to get your credit life back don't you think?

A word of advice here. If you owe the IRS and are receiving letters from them it would be a good idea to consult a tax attorney early in the game. The attorney if hired will step in between you and the IRS long before you are the target of any criminal action and in most cases can save you big money in fines and fees as well.

By using credit reporting as a tool the IRS gets to collect the money and punish you without a judge or jury in most cases. They even get to sentence you and once you make restitution, assuming you actually owed the money to begin with, they get to extend the sentence seven more years because you paid.

So how can you get a tax lien off your credit report? It's amazing how this question gets asked again and again for every type of problem. The premise stays the same, regardless of what the particular piece of adverse information is. **So let's go right to the details of the strategy** and show you how to remove it before or after it's paid.

First it is important to remember even though it's called a "tax lien", in reality it is still a judgment. A judgment for taxes is no different than a judgment for anything else. It is a complaint for a debt allegedly owed which results in lien or judgment against you. This usually happens because you didn't show up in court, therefore creating a "default" judgment in favor of the government.

NOTE: If you are served with a civil complaint for taxes or receive a notice of hearing regarding taxes contact a tax attorney. Don't ignore it and don't under any circumstance represent yourself in the matter. The government plays by a completely different set of rules and you can do yourself and your family quite a bit of damage by attempting to represent yourself pro se in a tax case. Be smart and seek professional guidance.

There is one good thing with respect to tax liens and the law when they are paid. The statute of limitations applies to paid tax liens. Meaning if you have a release of lien from the court and seven years has gone by the credit bureau must remove the tax lien from your credit report. So obviously one of the best strategies is to obtain a release of lien and put the credit bureau in a position where they have no choice but to remove it right?

But wait! What if you didn't pay the lien yet? Can you still obtain a release of lien from the IRS? Yep! There are many reasons why a lien can be legally released and only one has to do with money. For instance, what if it turned out you really didn't owe the money as alleged? What if you didn't owe as much as the original filing of the lien stated? What if the government can't prove what you owe when you challenge them?

A "removal" or "withdrawal" of a tax lien will get you what you need to have the bureau remove it from your credit report right away. In the FCRA Section 605(a)(3) it states "Paid tax liens which, from the date of payment, antedate the report by more than seven years". There is no mention of "removed" or "withdrawn tax liens.

Most of us believe that once someone has a judgment or lien against them it is too late to correct the problem. Remember, through the law there is almost always a way out because our system is set up to protect us from unwarranted and unproven allegations, mistakes, fraud or cases where new evidence arises after the fact. Even when we make mistakes there is a way to correct them from causing permanent damage.

Remember there are always options available. On the IRS.gov web site they post the following regarding the removal or withdrawal of a tax lien. There is also the "offer in compromise" strategy for those of you who owe and want to setup a payment plan but again I highly recommend letting a tax attorney negotiate this for you. Using a CPA (certified public accountant) or some tax company like H&R Block etc… may be cheaper and convenient but a lawyer provides two critical things. An attorney can offer expertise on taxes and the law as well as a layer of protection as any documents or conversations you have with your attorney are protected under "attorney / client privilege" where with an accountant that protection doesn't exist.

Ok, let's move on. "The IRS will withdraw a Notice of Federal Tax Lien if the Notice was filed while a bankruptcy automatic stay was in effect. The IRS may withdraw a Notice of Federal Tax Lien if the IRS determines that…

(1) The Notice was filed too soon or not according to IRS procedures.

(2) You enter into an installment agreement to satisfy the liability unless the installment agreement provides otherwise.

(3) Withdrawal will allow you to pay your taxes more quickly.

(4) Withdrawal is in your best interest, as determined by the National Taxpayer Advocate, and the best interest of the government" IRS.gov; www.irs.gov/taxtopics/tc201.html

You don't necessarily need a release to effect the removal of a tax lien from your credit report. When we discussed the "two point match" we found out the credit bureaus use a system to validate a debt no matter what type. If the lien isn't in the right name, address, and social security number or if the case numbers do not match up you have a legitimate argument the lien does not belong to you.

Remember, the fact you may have owed money does not in and of itself mean the account or other adverse information was reported in accordance with the law. This is business ladies and gentlemen, there is no room for feelings until later when you have the opportunity to straighten things out or prove your point in court.

Please also keep in mind that removing a tax lien from your credit report will not by itself relieve you of the debt. Unless the lien is released, satisfied or withdrawn for legal reasons or by the IRS you will still eventually have to deal with it and should do so as soon as humanly possible in order to avoid any further interruptions of your financial life. By the way, the IRS has many different plans to negotiate a debt without you getting killed in interest and fees. The most common of these is called "offer and compromise".

Like everything else there is a right way and a wrong way to do this. The wrong way is to let the government do it for you. The right way is to hire the services of an attorney or at minimum an accountant with a CPA who will not only draw up the offer but do the negotiating for you. Remember that with a tax attorney you are completely protected under attorney client privilege.

Don't negotiate with the IRS by yourself. You may think you can do just as good job as anyone else but a tax attorney will be able to eliminate fees and interest in most cases. I'm not talking about one of those companies you see running commercials on television. I am referring to a lawyer in your area who only represents clients on tax related issues. Big difference!

There will be a fee of course but their fee is usually far outweighed by the money they save you in interest, fees, and penalties. Just one good example is the fact they can work out a payment arrangement over an extended period of time where the interest is frozen or eliminated throughout the duration of the program.

That alone is worth its weight in gold. Regardless of how the lien is resolved please remember when you remove information from your credit report it does not necessarily absolve you of the debt.

In other words, the credit bureaus are not the creditors, government or collection agency so removing information from their system doesn't free you of the debt unless the creditor violated the law in some way or failed to comply with it.

Go on the web and find a tax attorney or CPA in your area. A piece of advice if I may… The most successful people in the world have one common thread between them. They surround themselves with the best professionals in each given field for which they themselves do not have expertise. You don't have to be rich to subscribe to this theory, just smart enough to use it.

STUDENT LOANS – Resources and Strategy for Deleting

In my opinion, one of the biggest problems we face as a nation is the problem of education and paying for it. It's one of those issues everyone agrees on but few are willing to take a stand on. Some food for thought…

1) Student loan debt will exceed 1 Trillion Dollars in 2012 which is more than the total outstanding for credit card debt.
2) Almost 15% of students default within 3 years of making their first student loan payment.
3) Since 1978 the cost of college has gone up over 900%.
4) Approximately 2/3 of all college students will graduate with a minimum debt of $25,000.00
5) Nearly half of twenty-somethings have stopped paying a debt, forcing lenders to "charge off" the debt and sell it to a collection agency, or had cars repossessed or sought bankruptcy protection

Children living in the Caribbean speak three and four languages living in an environment scarcely better than some of America's worst ghettos. The Japanese, Chinese, Germans and other countries teach their children to speak English at a very young age because they know children are the key to their country's future and we are their number one customer.

Consider the over-all effect of this issue. We go to college but it costs more than we or our families can afford. Before we've completed our education we accumulate 10s of thousands in debt. We get out of college and start looking for a job to begin our lives and to pay off the student loans and credit card debt we accumulated while there. Our first job is rarely a high paying one so we're in the 30k – 45k range. After taxes and living expenses we can barely make the student loan payment.

This puts us in a tough financial position where we end up choosing what debts to pay. Eventually our credit cards suffer and then the student loans. Once we realize our credit is destroyed we throw in the towel because we don't know how to deal with it all. You start thinking college was a waste of time. Most feel overwhelmed and very few know how to deal with the consequences of the foregoing events. We hide from the debt collectors and get angry when our tax refund is taken by the IRS.

Here's the question; is this the way we want our young people to start their lives? If you begin your adult life in debt, angry, embarrassed and confused where do you think you're likely to end up in your thirties or later on? G-d forbid you fall in love, get married and procreate. Now there are more mouths to feed and those old debts become even less important to you vs. little things like food, electric, phone, car and so on.

As a nation we spent over 500 Billion Dollars to bail out the savings and loan industry in the 80s and over 1 trillion in the Great Recession bailing out banks, AIG and others Why? Because the government decided they were important pillars to the American economy and future. If we took just 1% of that money and put it in an interest bearing account, we could send every child to private school and then off to Ivy League colleges with no debt on the way out forever.

Someone once called me a "liberal" directed as a character flaw. My family laughs at this perception because they consider me to be one of the most conservative people in their lives. However, if it makes me a liberal to want to see tax dollars go towards the education of our kids as opposed to the bailing out of banks, other nations and politicians then slap that label on and I'll wear it proudly.

Don't get me wrong; banks and foreign aid are important issues and deserving of assistance under certain circumstances but not at the expense of our kids. They grow up to be our leaders. Ok, Sorry for the side bar. I'll step off the soap box now.

So what do we do when we're shackled with student loan debt, credit cards and car loans coming straight out of the incubator of modern life? What are the options in terms of repayment, loan forgiveness, bad debt, taxes and the law?

On March 8, 2012 Congressman Hansen Clarke (D-Mich.) introduced H.R. 4170, the Student Loan Forgiveness Act of 2012. This law is focused on three primary solutions. The first, to create a 10/10 loan repayment plan. A 10% cap on borrower's discretionary income to establish the monthly payment amount for 10 years after which the loan or loans can be forgiven under certain circumstances.

The forgiveness provision kicks in after a borrower makes 120 payments, which must be either payment under the 10/10 plan; payments that were not less than they would have been under the 10/10 plan; or "payments" of $0 during a month the borrower was in deferment due to an economic hardship.

Secondly it will help student loan borrowers by capping Interest rates at 3.4%. After July of this year (2012) the rate is supposed to increase to 6.8%. If the bill is passed it will stay at 3.4%. Thirdly the act would also provide for Public Service Loan Forgiveness after 60 monthly payments instead of 120. Qualifying public service employment is full-time paid work in the government; a 501(c)(3) nonprofit; an AmeriCorps or Peace Corps position; or for a private "public service organization. (Source = U.S. news and world report, January 5, 2011)

Lastly some eligible borrowers would be able to obtain a Federal Consolidation loan to discharge private loans. There is a petition you can sign on to if you review the proposed law (H.R. 4170) and feel you would like to support it. To participate you can go to Signon.org. There is a link to the "Student Loan Forgiveness Act of 2012" on the home page. You can apply for Stafford Loan forgiveness if you serve in the AmeriCorps for 12 months.

You can contact them at 1.800.942.2677. The Peace Corps offers possible deferment of Stafford, Perkins and Consolidation loans and partial cancellation of Perkins (15% for each year of service). You can contact the Peace Corps at 1.800.424.8580 or 202.692.1845. There is also the VISTA (Volunteers in Service to America) program offering $4,725.00 for every 1700 hours of service. To contact them call 1.800.942.2677 or 202.606.5000.

There are also Military and Teaching loan forgiveness programs. There are even programs for legal and medical studies. For legal programs you can contact 202.466.3686 and for medical 916.654.1833. Also hospitals and healthcare facilities may offer forgiveness programs for new recruits. More information on the issue of forgiveness and loan cancellation can be found on staffordloan.com. Click the "Student Loan Forgiveness" link on the left side menu.

The message of this section is to know the battlefield before you get in this mess. Plan for your child to get loans with the intention of service later to get some or all of those loans forgiven to lessen their financial burden upon leaving school and moving into the first phase of their adult lives. Most of all I want you to learn that there are always options available for any pickle you may be in.

You need to search for those solutions fitting your needs. Scholarships', Grants, Internships and loans should all be part of the family discussion when planning for college.

In the July of 2012 we will be releasing "Credit Warfare for Parents" which will be solely focused on educating parents, teen aged kids and college students as to how to prepare for, setup and insulate themselves from their new credit life.

It will show parents how to teach their children the proper strategies for developing and preparing for using credit while showing Mom and Dad how to protect themselves from getting hit when the kids avoid telling them about the payments they didn't make.

The most important thing to remember when trying to remove student loans from a credit report is there are allot of hands in the pot. What I mean is you initially got the loan from a lender who knows they are guaranteed payment by the government (federal or state).

If you have defaulted on those student loans collection agents get involved and then on occasion the account gets sent to an attorney. Lastly, we cannot forget the IRS. They are the instrument used on many occasions to collect the money for a defaulted student loan.

Does this sound confusing to you? We'll sort it out together and go over strategies for you to use in order to remove student loans from your credit report. Oh, remember you're not fighting the government when attempting to do this. Your fight is with the credit bureaus, lenders, and collection agents involved in the original loan, not the government.

Believe it or not, the IRS sees this service they provide for lenders as a big pain in the neck. It requires allot of paperwork for them and then there is always the uncomfortable reality of having to play the bad guy in the deal because they're the one taking the money from the tax refund you were counting the seconds to receive.

Regardless of how many hands are in the pot, student loans can be removed from your credit report. The key here is who did the reporting and what legal mistakes did they make. For instance, did they report a deferment after the default? Did they extend the reporting period by sending it to a collection agency or attorney? Did they inflate the debt without adjudication of a court or by contract?

These are important questions you must ask yourself before you attempt to remove a student loan from your credit report. The more hands or entities the loan has traveled through the more likely it is you will be able to get it removed from your credit report. **Quick reminder**; this does not necessarily absolve you of the debt.

Let's start with deferment. If the loan was deferred, or more importantly reported as deferred after it went into default, then it would be fair to argue the account never went into default to begin with. Sometimes individuals receive more than one deferment from the same source and they all appear on the credit report showing different dates of last activity.

This could lead a lender to believe you have more student loan obligations than you actually do. It could also work to your advantage in removing the defaulted ones from the report. Even though "date of last activity" is not a term used in the law, the credit bureaus use it as a marker of time. The advantage to this is we can use it to our advantage either way.

If the account is truly older than seven years and the date of last activity makes it seem to have been reported more recently we can use the "Back Door" strategy to force the bureau to remove it. If however the facts indicate that the date of last activity shows a deferment after a default we can argue the more recent notation is the true and accurate accounting of the loan. Remember, this is a process in which you are allowed to use whatever errors are made by either the bureau or the creditor to your advantage. **Keep your emotions out of it**.

The most important thing to remember about student loans is there are so many hands in the pot including the bank, the collection company, the attorney, and sometimes the government. As a result, many mistakes get made in the process of collecting and reporting the status of the account. You only need to win one battle to win the war.

You don't have to prove they are all wrong. In other words, if the bank can't prove the debt upon request or just refuses to reply to the bureau's request once initiated by you, then the credit bureau will remove the bank's notation of the defaulted student loan and leave the collection account and any other notations regarding the account.

The law says the reporting period for adverse information appearing on your credit report cannot be extended by a collection of the same debt. Meaning if you owe a bank $5,000.00 for a student loan which went into default in 2005, and a collection for the same loan was reported in 2011, The statute of limitations runs out at the end of seven years from the point when the bank closed the loan out in 2005, not when the collection company reported they have the account in 2011.

This plays a critical role in how information is removed from a credit report legally. Collection companies always get the account from the original lender and report it to the credit bureau on their own as if it were a whole separate issue. As a result, they have convinced the public they can keep information on a credit report for an indefinite amount of time by continuing to report it each New Year.

Not only is it illegal for them to do this but it shows another example of how creditors have no regard for the damage their mistakes cause. This applies to any type of account, not just student loans. Once you have removed the original lenders notation of the account or had it updated to a positive rating, you can force the credit bureau to remove the collection account which went along with it.

In the Federal Register under the interpretations for section 605 of the FCRA (Obsolete Information), it states unequivocally that "The reporting period is not extended by assignment to another entity for further collection, or by partial or full payment of the account". **NOTE:** A consumer's "repayment agreement" with the creditor or a collection agency may be treated as a new account that has its own seven year period. When I said earlier the law doesn't allow for recovering from these issues with your conscience intact and in fact punishes you by extending the reporting of it for an additional seven years this is what I was referring to.

Collection agencies create a repayment agreement. You sign not knowing the consequences and then suffer for another seven years. **Don't do this under any circumstance**. Most of you who have a problem with student loans are now in your late twenties or older and have collection agents and lawyers abusing your rights under this Act. If an attorney wants to go to court and get a judgment regarding the student loan, he or she may do so.

In the event they do get a judgment simply use the strategies discussed in the chapter on judgments. **It is always better to answer** the summons / complaint within the first 20 – 30 days your state allows. This gives you much more time to deal with the issue and takes away the easy out of a default judgment for the plaintiff. If you don't file an answer within your state's time frame (20 – 30 days) the court will issue a default judgment and your situation worsens.

There are other ways to get the student loan off of your credit report besides using section 605 of the FCRA. There is the "Two Point Match" chapter to guide you through using the credit bureau's own internal policies to get it removed. There is the "Back Door" as discussed earlier and there is some new information which has only now been made available to us.

The Clinton administration approved a bill in the 1990s creating (Direct Consolidation Loans) allowing you to refinance a student loan regardless of where you originally applied or who the lender was (private, state, or federal). It is without question one of the most important pieces of legislation related to student loans to come out of any administration in years.

Why? Because until this was done, you signed an agreement with the lender to start repaying your school loans when you got out of college and keep paying until the balance was paid in full. You may get loans from multiple lenders and need to make multiple payments under different terms and rates. By consolidating the loans into one loan with one rate and defined term you simplify the matter. You also remove the chance of multiple issues should you not be able to pay for a while or need a deferment and if it all goes bad you only have one entity you will be dealing with as relates to collection and or your credit. What if you couldn't get a job and were unable to pay the loan?

Well, you could file for a deferment of the loan for six months or so to buy some time. What if you still didn't have a decent job even though you've been trying hard to find one? Prior to these programs the answer was to not pay the loan until you finally got the job and were able to pay.

Under the DCL program and the *Special Direct Consolidation Loan Program* you can get all loans refinanced under one loan with better rates and terms as long as they are current or no more than 270 days past due.

Allowing student loan borrowers to default was definitely a bad strategy for the lenders because they have thrown into default hundreds of thousands of student loans over the last decade or so and as a result have caused a snowball effect of individuals who have bad credit before they ever got off the ground financially. So why would they do it?

Consider the environment. It's like an SBA loan for business. The loans are guaranteed by the government so the bank isn't concerned about what happens when you default. It becomes a government problem reported to the credit bureaus and later causing the IRS to take your tax refunds until the full amount is paid off.

Anyway, the United States government decided since they end up paying these loans for you only to be forced into taking your tax refund money as their only means of recovering the funds, it would be a good idea to extend an olive branch to the borrower. Creating programs to get the borrower to pay the loans off or have them forgiven later under certain circumstances is a better plan. So the Clinton, Bush and now Obama administration decided to create plans to recover these moneys in a friendlier manner.

The government will now buy your student loan from whoever is currently holding the note and refinance it for up to 30 years. They will take over the loan from the lender(s) and give you a choice of options to repay it.

In the past the government treated student loan defaults like tax evaders. As a result, millions of Americans were left hanging out to dry after college. Now they're trying to fix the federal budget deficit and in so doing have looked for ways to recoup moneys otherwise lost.

You can find details on the government web site for these programs (http://studentaid.ed.gov). Once you clear the defaults off your credit report you won't be hounded for this debt anymore and you'll have a new positive on your credit report.

FILE VARIATIONS – Strategic Advantage

When your name, address, social security number or other personal information is reported incorrectly to the bureaus identify these as "file variations". Experian used to call them "checkpoints", Equifax "AKA search", and Trans Union "Hawk Alert". Now they title these areas "Additional Information" or "Personal Information".

Regardless of what they call them they are very simply file variations (typos etc…) on your credit report. That is, somehow your name, address, ss#, or other piece of basic information gets mistyped or entered wrong and causes an alert to appear on your file which is meant to warn potential lenders you may be using different names, addresses etc...

That's right, even though these "variations" were through no fault of your own placed on your report, the bureaus have designed it to look like you intended for it to happen. Of course they didn't consider it may have been the creditors or collection agencies who made a mistake in entering your name or some other piece of identifying information or the lender where you applied when trying to pull the credit report in the first place.

This is where the credit bureaus get the 450 million files they boast having from. As mentioned previously, they claim they have 450 million files in their database when there are only a total of 202 million Americans alive with files of any kind. They then tell us the huge discrepancy is due to "overlapped / merged files". Those files they duplicated because their system isn't sure who it is.

As we discussed earlier in the "Two Point Match", these errors can be used to help you remove negative information from your credit report. However, once your report is clear from adverse information you do not want any of these alerts on there because they make it look like you're up to something fishy.

The good news is that whether you have one or more of these on your credit report they are relatively easy to remove. The bad news is that if they are left unattended they can cause a whole bunch of problems for you down the line. Even someone with just a similar last name as yours could get their file merged together with yours and cause you tons of aggravation.

The interesting part about this flaw in the credit bureau's software is it completely contradicts what the bureaus claim with regard to safeguarding your file from unwarranted abuse of creditors and others.

If they can't tell the difference between J. Smith in Brooklyn and J. Smith in Manhattan, how could they possibly claim they verified information from a dispute based solely on a phone call or email? I mean, how do they know the individual whom they are attempting to verify information on is in fact the individual the information belongs to or shouldn't for that matter?

It gets confusing doesn't it? That's ok; they can't figure it out either. While they're trying, we get to use it to our advantage when we need it, and have it cleared off when we don't. If you should look at your credit report and see one of these notations, all you need to do is send a letter to the credit bureau telling them this information, whether it's just a name spelling mistake or other error, is not who you are or where you live (d).

Send them something like a current electric bill to show the proper address and they must delete it post haste. This can also be done through the bureaus online dispute systems but remember to be very careful what checkboxes you hit in stating a reason for removing the information.

Once your credit is cleared up remove these remarks from your report and be sure to check once a year for these and other potentially damaging notations. You worked hard to get your financial life back, don't get lazy and let the credit bureaus mess it up for you while you're not looking.

From a credit repair stand point they can be very useful. For example if you have judgments or other court actions on your report and they show under (Robert Smith) but your formal name is Robert T. Smith you can use the two point match to remove those notations. The same holds true of they show a different address. Think about it; if they don't know the true address of an account how can they possibly verify it?

Make sure you leave these alternate names, addresses etc.. on your credit report until 100% of the negatives are deleted. They can and probably will prove to be a valuable resource throughout the process.

This is yet another reason why I don't want you to call the credit bureaus to dispute unless you are (a) following up on a previous attempt and (b) are absolutely certain you can control yourself when asked questions unrelated to the reason you called like questions about these file variations. Whenever possible conduct your business in writing and stay off the phone.

THE 100 WORD STATEMENT – Pointless or Useful?

Everyone in the credit galaxy will tell you; you have a right to put a 100 word statement on your credit report in the event you feel there is something being reported incorrectly or for some reason needs to be explained. Like when there is a bankruptcy or tax lien on your credit report. They tell you about this right of yours in a way that makes you believe if you put a statement on your credit report, future lenders will take it into consideration when deciding whether or not to extend a loan to you.

Sorry to bust your bubble but it just ain't so. Lenders see it as an admission of fact, not a reason to feel sorry for you and disregard it as an unfortunate incident in your life. This is the real world ladies and gentlemen, and in the real world unfortunately, nobody cares about mitigating circumstances but for a very few exceptions. Also these days with automated approvals and declines we are judged in an instant on our credit score and not a thorough review of the accounts in your file or mitigating circumstances as to why some may show negatively.

Now I know this doesn't make you feel all warm and fuzzy inside but that's not my job. Keep in mind they are looking for reasons to deny the loan, not reasons to grant it especially now during the great recession.

Still not warm and fuzzy? I can scarcely think of a circumstance where it would be productive to put a 100 word statement on your credit report unless you are absolutely certain it will do you no harm. You'll notice I didn't say unless you're certain it will help with the application?

That's because it would be impossible to know in advance without being a mind reader. Its damage you're looking to avoid which is what you need to consider when attempting to cure a potentially bad situation with an explanation.
You know the old saying, "excuses are like _____, everyone has one and they all stink"? Well that is precisely why explanations rarely work out as relates to credit.

However, if you're intent on doing this lets at least go over some of the different situations where it <u>may</u> be useful. **Remember** anything you write is going to be seen not only by potential lenders but employers, insurance companies, and anyone else who checks your credit.

If you're going to do this, do it in circumstances where it's in your best interest to admit or explain what happened. For instance, if you were the victim of a crime like someone stole your check book and wrote checks that ultimately came back because you had the account closed. Another instance might be when your credit report shows late payments and they were a direct result of the company whom you sent the payment to moving and not because you genuinely sent it late or when something shows up on your credit report that belongs to a family member.

Another circumstance might be when something was supposed to be covered by insurance like medical bills and they sent it to collections while you were haggling with the insurance company who ultimately paid the debt.

In these circumstances it would probably behoove you to put a 100 word statement on your report so future lenders not only understand what happened but can see it either is or will be resolved in your favor. Like a bankruptcy which shows on your credit report as "Dismissed".

If something belongs to a family member you can explain it through the 100 word statement and give the family member's name so they can check it out. That is of course if you want to give their name up to a potential creditor.

If the negative accounts ended up there by mistake, the other family member should have no qualms about helping you straighten it out. If they do, get a new family member immediately! Just kidding, well maybe not.

Sometimes companies move just like people and as a result payments may get registered late when they weren't. If this happens to you don't fret, just get letter head from company with their new address and show it to any potential lender who may inquire. In the meantime it won't harm you to put a statement regarding these facts on your credit report.

Lastly, when something is supposed to be covered by insurance and the insurance company doesn't pay right away like you thought they were going to; often times the hospitals and doctors send the debts to collection agents who put those collection accounts on your credit report. If the insurance company later pays the bill, the collector must by law remove the collection account from your credit report. While all of this is going on, a statement of the facts will probably suffice in calming any nervous lenders.

But be prepared for if and possibly when the future creditor to whom you are applying asks for documentation to back up the statement.

NOTE: I would prefer you do not place a 100 word statement on your credit report at all. If you are concerned about perception of debt by a future creditor or employer you can draft a letter and attach it to the application vs. making it part of the bureaus records.

DATE OF LAST ACTIVITY – Is It Legal?

On your credit report you may see dates appearing for individual accounts that have what the credit bureaus call a "date of last activity or transaction". The account is kept on your report from this date for seven years according to the credit bureaus. They use this as a marker of time in order to judge when an account should come off your credit report.

There's one major problem with this policy, it's illegal. That's right; there is no mention in the Fair Credit Reporting Act of "date of last activity or transaction" as a marker of time for the seven year reporting period. The credit bureaus created this as the starting date for any account being reported in a negative way because often they have no idea when it was "charged off to profit and loss", "adjudicated" or "closed". They have convinced most lenders this is the date to look at when attempting to decipher how long ago a person's problems occurred.

Bankers, mortgage brokers, real-estate agents, finance managers, and anyone else who pulls credit reports in order to do business with us are convinced this is when the seven year period begins. As a result, accounts which should be long gone from your credit report may still be sitting there.

For the record, the law, which is the only thing that matters, says adverse information stays seven years from the "date charged off to profit and loss" or the "date of adjudication" as the case may be. In the case of bankruptcy as we discussed earlier, it is ten years from the "date of entry of the order for relief" or the "date of adjudication". There is no phrase, inference or other notation which would lead any prudent person to interpret the language in the law as validating "date of last activity" or "date of last transaction".

The law says *"upon the expiration of the 180-day period beginning on the **date of the commencement of the delinquency** which immediately preceded the collection activity, charge to profit and loss, or similar action"*. Big difference wouldn't you say?

This is one of the most important pieces of evidence the credit bureaus know their only value lies in their ability to maintain negative information in credit files and then present themselves as savior to their corporate customers.

Once again I remind you of the value of the Back Door strategy. By disputing the debt and requiring proof you request among other things evidence of the "date of the commencement of the delinquency". You would request proof of not only that there was a delinquency but exactly when it first occurred.

What if the report shows your account reported as of June 1st but the account went delinquent in November of the previous year? The law says 180 days later it can be reported making April 1st the date it should be reported as having gone delinquent.

If you feel guilty about disputing your credit report because you feel like you owe the money remember you are not disputing morality here. You are disputing accuracy, time lines and verification capability and are not debating in court or elsewhere whether or not you transacted and or owed as reported.

Why do you suppose the bureau describes the creditor or collection agency a "subscriber" anyway? The bottom line is the word "subscriber" equals or is a synonym for "customer". To get customers you need to convince your market you have something of value.

The files with good credit are certainly of value however those with bruised credit are of more value because they save the creditor from taking on an unnecessary risk.

If the system worked as originally envisioned and was fair those objectives would sit fine with me. Unfortunately the system is seriously flawed and consumers need to know how it truly works and how to manage their credit lives with all the known tools available. Anyway, if you should end up in a big dog fight over the seven year thing just revert back to the "Back Door" chapter and slam dunk those guys once you either have the proof or lack thereof.

COLLECTION AGENTS AND THE FDCPA – Fear Not!

In this section we're going to focus on the debt collection, the Fair Debt Collection Practices Act (FDCPA), how it works, how it affects you and how the law protects you from unfair and illegal practices perpetrated by collection agents. Most people at one time or another have run into some financial difficulty, usually do to a circumstance they, for whatever reason, could not control. Soon after the accounts are closed by the creditor, collection agents start calling and sending letters demanding payment of the debt.

Most of these collection agents are completely unprofessional and abusive when they contact you. They rely solely on fear and intimidation tactics to try to force you to pay a bill either you obviously can't afford or perhaps don't owe. This is the main reason the "Fair Debt Collection Practices Act" was enacted on September 20th, 1977.

Congress realized these companies used cruel and unfair methods to frighten people into paying bills they may not have owed adding bogus interest and fees to the debt without legal justification. The law was written to protect us from these unscrupulous companies and to provide relief from the undue pressure created by them.

In the following pages we'll discuss several important sections of this law and how they relate to your current situation. We will also show you how, with minimal effort, you can stop these collection agents from harassing you and actually put them on the defensive.

Before we begin, let's first have an understanding of how these companies function and what motivates them to behave the way they do. We'll also discuss a little history about debt collection and how it relates to the present day.

Years ago when a person owed a debt, the original creditor would try to collect the money on their own or send it to an attorney. It was more cost effective back then to handle receivables in-house instead of contracting someone to do it for you. In the last 40 years or so the population has grown and the amount of people using credit to leverage their version of the American dream has grown exponentially. Therefore, it is no longer cost affective for most companies to do their own collecting.

In the early seventies, collection companies began to multiply. They feed off of the dead files that big banks and other lenders store away. You see, big companies could not both grow and collect at the same time, or at least they didn't want to have to do both. So they concentrated their efforts on building their customer base and let somebody else worry about the people that didn't pay. Businesses figured out that the majority of their accounts at any given time are current, so why should they spend valuable time and money chasing the few when they could be profiting off the many.

It was the perfect marriage, the credit grantor and the credit collector. Collection companies act on behalf of the original creditor and attempt to collect the moneys owed, plus some interest and fees they may or may not be entitled to. Unfortunately, they began to use some pretty cruel methods in order to achieve their goal. Finally, after thousands of complaints to the F.T.C., Congress enacted the "Fair Debt Collection Practices Act" or FDCPA.

This law was designed to lay the ground rules for collection agents, collection attorneys and collection departments of large corporations to follow, and believe me, the collection agents lobbied hard against it and hate it now. It was much more fun for them when there were no rules to follow.

Most of them still disregard the law unless you remind them of it and are willing to do something about it. This section will show you what to do and how to do it.

Before you can understand how to deal with collection agents, you must first understand how their business works and what motivates them. Most collection agencies buy outstanding debt or invoices from the original creditor or get it on consignment at a discounted price. They then chase you for the total amount of the money plus interest and fees, and if they succeed they get to keep their share.

When I say they buy or get the invoice on consignment I mean they pay a discounted price for it either way and whatever they collect in the case of a purchased account or invoice they get to keep. In the case of an invoice given to them on consignment they get a percentage of what they collect. The more they collect, the more they make. The more people they call and harass, the more they collect.

It's nothing more than a numbers game, with your financial life hanging in the balance. The only thing that matters to them is the money, nothing more, nothing less. They don't care that you got sick, laid off, divorced or anything else. They want the money plain and simple and they'll usually go to almost any length to get it.

As I stated earlier there is no point telling them your tales of woe, they will only make you feel worse by saying something to make you feel guilty or incompetent. They'll try to make you feel inferior by speaking to you in a condescending fashion. They'll try to scare you by telling you they'll garnish your wages or get a judgment against you and put a lien against your home. It seems like they'll stop at nothing to collect a debt and never lose any sleep over their unethical methods.

The only productive way to deal with these companies is to set your mind to a war mentality. By war mentality I mean you can't afford to let your emotions get involved. You should take the attitude this is strictly business and nothing more. If you allow them to plant the seeds of guilt and shame in you, the only result will be depression and a counterproductive outcome.

They only make money if they collect money so the motivation is pretty strong for them to break the rules, hence "*Credit Warfare*". The only way to stop feeling guilty and weak is to have a clear understanding of what your rights are. **So let's begin** there.

You have the right to have any debt proven to you regardless of what the collector says or how much you think or they say you may owe (FDCPA Section 809(b). As discussed earlier in the *Back Door* chapter, if you make the request for proof of the debt in writing, they must provide proof of the debt to you.

From the moment they receive your dispute letter they must "cease collection of the debt" (FDCPA 809(b). If they fail to acquire and provide the proof you requested, they must cease collection of the debt forever. If the collector, attorney or creditor fails to provide all of the proofs requested in writing they cannot continue any other collection efforts.

In a staff response letter from the FTC to an attorney regarding this issue the FTC dated March 3, 1992 the FTC stated the following.

*"Section 809(b) of the Act provides that if the consumer disputes the debt or requests identification of the original creditor in writing, the collector **must cease collection efforts until he verifies the debt**, or identifies the original creditor and mails a response to the consumer. If the consumer's request for verification of the debt was made in accordance with Section 809(b) of the Act, the collector need not supply the documentation but only so long as collection efforts are not resumed. Section 809(b) requires that "**the collector cease collection of the debt**, or any disputed portion thereof, **until the debt collector obtains verification** of the debt . . . and a copy of such verification . . . is mailed to the consumer by the debt collector." In situations contemplated by Section 809(b**), the Act imposes the obligation to furnish verification before the collector resumes collection efforts**. In the event the collector decides not to pursue the collection efforts, there is no requirement to furnish the documentation of the indebtedness to the consumer. In the event that collection efforts are resumed, the requirement to furnish verification to the consumer prior to resumption of collection remains"*

This is probably the most important part of the FDCPA because it gives you the ability to put the collector on the defensive before they even get a chance to harass you and disrupt your life.

Once you dispute the debt "all" collection activity must cease. That means no more calls, collection letters, threats, law suits etc… You have many other rights you should be aware of under this law and how to enforce them if necessary.

1] No debt collector can call someone else, like a neighbor or employer, and discuss the fact that you owe any money. (FDCPA Section 804 (2)

2] They cannot send mail which indicates they are in the debt collection business to anyone except you. (Section 804 (5))

3] If you are represented by an attorney, they cannot contact anyone else except the attorney. (Section 804 (6)

4] They cannot contact you before 8:00am and after 9:00pm anywhere. (Section 805(1).

5] It is illegal for them to even try to contact any third party in connection with a debt without your prior written consent. (Section 805 (3)(b)

6] If you notify the debt collector in writing that you will not pay the debt or you simply wish to never be contacted again, they must immediately stop contacting you except to notify you of some other action or remedy they intend to take, like going to court. (Section 805(3)(c)

This section is crucial for your sanity because it gives you the right to stop them cold simply by sending a letter, certified mail, stating you want them never to call you again at home or any other location and that all further correspondence will be done through the mail. From that point forward, they must do business through the mail and the mail only. (Section 805(3c)

7] They cannot threaten you, your property, or your reputation. (Section 806(1). Remember, saying they are going to ruin your credit is threatening you and your reputation.

8] They cannot use obscene or profane language. (Section 806(2)

9] They can't use the telephone to harass by calling again and again. (Section 806(5). Did you know the telephone company has a service which allows you to enter a code on your telephone to stop numbers you designate from calling you? Check it out!

10] They can't misrepresent themselves as an attorney. (Section 807(3)

11] They can't make you feel like a criminal. (Section 807(7). If they use language which would lead a prudent person to feel like they were calling them a criminal they are in violation of the law.

12] They cannot report to the credit bureau any information which is false or should be known to be false, or fail to tell them that a debt is disputed by you. (Section 807(8). **This one is big** when considering the "Back Door" chapter. Once they have failed to prove the debt it "should be known to be false".

13] They can't use a false business name. (Section 807(14)

14] They can't ask for a postdated check, then deposit it when they're not supposed to in order to have it bounce and then threaten you with criminal prosecution. (Section 808(3). **Note to self**; never give a postdated check to anyone.

15] If you request written verification of the debt, they must provide it within 30 days. If they fail, they must cease collection of the debt. (Section 809(A/B)

16] If they are in consistent violation of the law, they are subject to a fine of $500,000 or 1% of their net worth, whichever is less. (Section 813(b)

Please pay close attention to these sections of the Debt Collection Practices Act, this law is written for your protection. If you understand your rights and how to enforce them, you'll never take a drastic step like filing a bankruptcy unless it's absolutely necessary.

Remember, most people file bankruptcy for all the wrong reasons. They usually do it because they want to end the pressure of collection agents and creditors calling or for fear of their paycheck or bank account being garnished.

The FDCPA is an extremely powerful tool to stop the harassment and protect yourself from garnishment without the stress, cost and humiliation of bankruptcy. In most cases bankruptcy is not the answer.

You know the old adage, *"The pen is mightier than the sword"*. Nothing could be more true when dealing with collection companies. This is not a time to be lazy, if you run from them you'll be running forever.

DEBT NEGOTIATION – Credit Repair Aside

When we discuss the negotiation of debt you first have to decide what your goal is. For instance, you may just want to negotiate a re-payment plan in order to get the collector to stop calling and harassing you each day (if this is your only goal, you can stop the harassing calls before you negotiate as discussed earlier).

You might want to try to pay off the debt and in so doing pay less than the original principal amount. Maybe you want to facilitate the dismissal of a lawsuit or the satisfaction of one. Regardless of what your particular agenda is you first have to understand all negotiation pivots on one word, "Leverage".

Negotiating is not for the faint of heart or emotional types. If you handle it wrong you could end up paying much more than you actually owed. You might even cause your credit to be damaged for a longer period of time as discussed earlier.

As I have stated all throughout this book your personal feelings are not relevant here, only your goal matters. You can of course custom tailor your goal to fit your feelings, but beware; money and credit often leave scars on our personal feelings.

Leverage is the key element to any negotiation. Leverage is having something the other party wants or fears enough that when brought to their attention will motivate them to compromise in your favor. Yes, a compromise can still be to one side or another's advantage. Leverage gives you the ability to persuade the opponent your offer is in their best interest.

You can't negotiate when you are upset or angry. You can't negotiate when you're frightened or threatened. You can only negotiate when you're calm and confident in what you are about to propose to the other side. In order to be calm and confident you need certain elements in place. For one thing it would help if you had the money for whatever amount you intend to try and settle it for ready in a lump sum.

It is a good idea to be aware of what the original amount owed was (principal amount), and that you are speaking to a person who can not only be persuaded but has the power to make the decision. The primary leverage anyone has when negotiating with creditors is money and legal position. If you are positioned correctly from a legal standpoint and have funds available at the time you contact them your chances for success increase many fold.

In any negotiation regarding money you first have to overcome the fear and guilt a creditor tries to use to get what they want. In other words you need to control your temper while not letting the other side lose theirs. You can't be intimidated by their voice or talking to you in a condescending fashion. You can't tolerate someone telling you the obvious like, "you had the responsibility of paying this debt to begin with" or "if you don't pay the way we say we'll _____".

You should be completely prepared for anything they might say and or want and not hope it goes your way simply because you're reaching out to them. Being prepared means anticipating their every move and having a counter move for it. It means knowing what you can and can't make happen on your end. Preparation means never being surprised or shocked at the response or lack thereof from your adversary. "He who is prepared and lies in wait for the enemy will be victorious" *Sun Tzu - The Art of War*.

Though it's called a negotiation it is in fact a war of will and leverage, your will against theirs. It always seems like their will is unbreakable when you are the one who owes, but that's just an illusion. When you contact them you should always look and or sound like you're broke. You never let them think you have extra money or things for you are just wonderful. If you do the enemy will be immovable and unrelenting. They will want the entire amount plus fees and interest regardless of whether they are entitled to it or not. They will threaten you twice as much and for ten times as long if they think you have the money.

They will hire lawyers and private investigators to poke into your life and find the money they think you have hidden from them. They may attempt to get a garnishment against your pay and or bank accounts. They will file lawsuits against you and force you to sit through a deposition where they ask you every question they can think of about your life and if you lie or refuse to answer they can cause you more trouble as in a contempt of court citation from the participating judge.

Are you getting the picture here? Never tell them where you work, how much you make, where you bank, whether or not you are married, if you own or rent, if you have any investments, savings accounts or other assets. Never make a payment agreement with any creditor who will not agree in writing in advance to *delete* the negative notation from your credit report permanently.

Don't even tell them how many kids you have or if you have any credit cards. Lastly, never assume they know anything about your life. They may act is if they do making you feel it's no big deal to volunteer information as if they actually had it.

Remember, your objective here may be to pay off an old debt but like a festering wound an old debt can become an infection or worse. What makes it worse is not being prepared or knowing how to handle the negotiating process. Worse still would be volunteering information the collector will use to make the wound worse for you like adding interest and fees that were not called for in the original contract.

Never deal or negotiate with anyone who is not a supervisor or in management. Don't get tricked into speaking to someone who identifies themselves as a "senior collector" or "manager". Make sure it's a supervisor or owner of the agency so your valuable time isn't wasted. One way you can be sure they are a supervisor is to ask for their last name. Most other collectors won't give their last name over the phone. Gee, I wonder why? Maybe it's because they're cruel to others and fear retribution.

It's important to remember to only speak to a supervisor because only a supervisor will be able and willing to help you if you have the money to resolve or "settle" the debt. Additionally a supervisor knows they can and should agree to remove the collection from your credit report if you pay the debt in full. The only problem is getting them to put it in writing.

That's the real trick in any negotiation with a debt collector. It's unfortunate but you simply cannot take their word for it. They will lie without hesitation to get the money. They know you have no recourse if they don't come through as promised. That's right! You can't sue them or get them fired or anything else for not deleting the collection from your credit report if you didn't get that commitment in writing in advance.

It's so important you remember this part because these people are not friends of yours or mine. Well, there definitely not friends of mine. They get paid an hourly wage plus incentives for collecting on debts. It's those incentives not to mention the biggest one, keeping their job that motivates them to behave in this fashion. **Get it in writing first or no deal!**

Once you have the right person on the phone the first thing you need to ask them for is proof of the principal amount of the debt when they first got the account or in the case of the original creditor when they closed the account.

If you're dealing with a collection agent, ask for what the principal amount of the debt was when the account was first closed by the creditor. Then send letter number eleven to the original creditor yourself and compare the two figures.

You should only negotiate to pay the principal amount owed at the time the account was closed. Of course you can pay less than that but you need a starting point that works to your advantage not theirs.

Why would they be willing to take less than the principal amount owed on the debt you ask? When your account was closed the original creditor eventually wrote the account off as bad debt on their taxes for that quarter. In addition, they may be insured for such a loss or possibly you signed for the insurance on the original application. On top of all that they sell the right to collect on the old debt to a collection agent for anywhere from .20 to .50 cents on the dollar or more. They never lose!

When you know the true principal amount of the debt on the day the account was closed you now have your starting point. The first question you ask the creditor is "What payoff figure are you offering if this debt is paid tomorrow"?

After you ask this question you shut up and don't speak until there is an answer. **This is very important**; you must not say anything once you've asked this question until they answer you. In sales, all sales people are or should be taught that once you ask a closing question you shut up, the next one who speaks loses, every time.

The reason for this is the element of control. If you are asking the questions and they are answering them you are controlling the conversation. If you're controlling the conversation you're controlling the negotiation as well. Believe me, they'll offer something lower than the principal amount almost immediately. They'll say something like "Well if you guarantee to pay tomorrow I'll except X dollars less".

Don't get excited, this is just the beginning of the negotiation not the end of it. The next thing you tell them is you would like them to contact the original creditor and see how much better they can do. You must justify in their mind why you didn't accept their original offer as well as why they should follow through with your request to contact the original creditor for a lower figure.

Here's the perfect answer to that question. " I only have so many dollars available and several creditors to cover, you are the most important so I called you first but you need to do better in order for me to pull this off" or something along those lines.

Remember your goal is twofold and theirs isn't. You want to pay off the debt with as little money as possible and have your credit record cleared. They want one thing and one thing only, the money.

Key Points to Remember:

1) **Always send letter 11** to each creditor and collection agency before you consider calling to negotiate. If they don't comply you are in complete control because the law says they must cease collection of the debt. Your calling to offer a settlement past that point is a generous move on your part as you are not legally obligated assuming they didn't comply.

2) If you can **conduct the negotiations in writing** and avoid speaking to anyone on the phone you will be far better off. This avoids any spontaneous screw ups in a fluid conversation.

3) **Don't call to negotiate** if you don't know in advance how much money you can part with in one shot. Calling to negotiate without the money in place and a plan will only irritate the creditor and make you look foolish.

4) **NEVER** sign a "repayment agreement" with a creditor or collection agency unless it states in writing that upon receipt of final payment the account will be "deleted" or "removed" from your credit file.

5) **Keep your emotions in check**. If you don't think you can on a given day then don't contact anyone. Wait for a day when your head's in the right place and you are calm.

   "He who is prepared and arrives on the field of battle first will be victorious" *Sun Tzu*. In other words. Have your act together before you call and expect everything. If you do you'll be able to stay calm throughout.

PREVENTIVE MEDICINE – Plan, Insulate, Protect

In any undertaking the best strategy is to prepare in advance for all possibilities. In light of this I have added this section on preventive medicine to give those of you who invested in this book some preventive strategies to save yourselves from as much pain as possible.

Preventive medicine is just that, a strategy by which you can prevent some adverse event from taking place namely damage to your credit reports, bank accounts, reputation, and sanity. Yes even your state of mind should be considered when we discuss preventive strategies because if your head is in the right place your less likely to make bad decisions regarding other issues. Your state of mind is how you are feeling at a particular time based on current or future conditions. For instance, how do you feel when a debt collector calls, when you see a new car you want, when you receive collection letters, when you speak to credit bureaus and collection agents?

In order to control your state of mind you first have to understand the problem you are or will be facing. If you are currently in a situation where your credit is good but financial problems are just around the corner there are many things you can do to prevent yourself from having to feel depressed or embarrassed. **Key Point** – Knowledge equals a feeling of control which helps maintain a calm and focused state of mind.

Contacting your creditors before the debt gets into the hands of a collection agent is a good strategy because when speaking to the original creditor you know going in they have the authority and flexibility to work with you towards a solution before it all goes bad.

They will work with you before they charge off the account and send it to an outside collection agency. Knowing what to do in every situation gives you piece of mind and allows you to make the appropriate decisions in your family's best interest.

What follows is a Q & A for every most scenarios. If you think of a new scenario you feel should be added here please feel free to either communicate with us through twitter (@ credit warfare) or on Facebook - http://facebook/creditwarfare.

Q. What if I lost my job and I need to buy time to get back on my feet?

A. First remember if you have to make a late payment on anything, date the check for the date the payment was actually due. For instance, if your payment is due on the 1st of January and you're paying on the 17th of February date the check 1/1/2012 and send it in. This gives you a canceled check dated from the due date which down the line could be very useful with respect to your credit reports.

Second call the original creditor as soon as trouble is on the horizon. When you call keep a few things in mind. First they will report the late payments regardless of what arrangements you make with them or what they tell you on the phone. Second you should have a clear plan in mind for negotiating with them before you call. If you don't have the money at all tell them when you anticipate you will.

In most cases they will avoid charging the account off as bad debt for the time frame you mention if the amount of time is reasonable. Third remember everything you say to them will be typed into their computer and if the account gets sent to a collection agent so might the transcript. Lastly ask what deferment, re-aging or forbearance programs they have.

Another strategy when you feel things are going to take a turn for the worse and you won't be able to make the payments as required. If your credit is currently good and you have truly caught this problem before it affected your credit (usually before late notices or calls start coming) you have several other options available to you. You could get one or two new major credit cards and move all the debts on your current ones to them which does two things. It reduces ten or more potential credit problems down to one or two, and usually the new bank will allow a grace period before payments begin.

You can also do this with a second mortgage, or personal loan. The idea is to minimize your exposure to credit problems by minimizing the number of creditors with whom you are currently indebted to. If your credit goes bad after that you are only dealing with one or two problems instead of a dozen or so.

Q. What if I'm behind on my car or mortgage payments?

A. In the chapters on foreclosures and repos we discussed moving the payments to the end of the note. You ask the lender to take the payments due and maybe one or two future payments (if properly motivated) and put those at the end of the loan. They will usually charge you an interest payment at the time you make this arrangement. This is a very practical and cost effective strategy for saving the car or house you love. This process is called "re-aging" the loan.

Q. What law covers charges showing on a credit card statement that are not mine?

A. The Fair Credit Billing Act governs such a situation. If a charge shows up you are not familiar with or are sure isn't yours you need to call, email through your online account or send a letter to the credit card company disputing the charge.

If you send using U.S. mail make sure you send it certified mail return receipt requested. They have 90 days in which to prove the charge is yours or remove it. If they claim they proved it you have 10 days from the point you receive notice to cure the debt.

Q. I just went through a divorce; can I prevent my ex-spouse from damaging my credit?

A. Yes you can. First send a letter certified mail return receipt requested to each of your creditors notifying them you are divorced and will not be responsible for the other's debt. If you were the original applicant and your ex-spouse was simply a duplicate card holder they will force the ex-spouse to apply for their own cards. If you were the duplicate card holder they can't hold you responsible anyway but send the letter just to be safe. If it was a vehicle both of you signed for you need to let the lien holder know to refinance the note in your name or theirs as the case may be. The same applies to a house.

Q. I am getting married or just did what should we do to protect ourselves credit wise?

A. If you are married, getting married, or just have a significant other there is one very simple rule to protect yourself from getting hurt in the future. Never apply for anything or fill out anything together.

All too often when you do the two files will be merged by the credit bureaus and if one of you gets sick or loses your job or some other unfortunate situation should arise it will affect both of you thereby taking away the safety net of having a backup credit file in the other person. Additionally should the relationship dissolve the previous Q & A would be a moot point.

Q. Can I stop the harassing phone calls without filing a Bankruptcy?

A. I'm glad you asked. Filing a bankruptcy in most cases is like using a ballistic missile to kill an ant. Most people file for all the wrong reasons. As we stated earlier, if you have no assets to protect you should not in my opinion file bankruptcy. If it's the depressing phone calls you're trying to avoid the answer is simple. You amend letter 11 and use only the part pertaining to phone calls.

Remember, section 805 of the FDCPA which pertains to communication in connection with a debt says if you notify the creditor not to contact you by telephone they can't. Always send this letter certified mail return receipt requested.

Q. What if a collection agency sends a letter or calls threatening to ruin my credit?

A. First of all, just the fact they mentioned ruining your credit is a violation of law. However in order to prevent them from doing so before you've had a chance to do something about it here is some strong preventive medicine. Get a supervisors name at the collection agency. Send them a letter (certified return receipt) stating the debt is being disputed and not to report it to any credit bureau until they prove the debt to you first (FDCPA sec 807 #8).

Make sure you tell them you will be checking your credit file to see they complied and all communication is to be conducted through the mail only. Do not ever let them drag you into a conversation about the alleged debt. Stick to your request for proof as directed in FDCPA sec 809(a)(b).

Q. Do I have to sign personally for everything I lease or buy for my business?

A. Yes and No. Experian and Dun & Bradstreet maintain corporate credit files. If you are in business you should make sure you have a file with one or both of them in order to avoid having to sign personally. The advantage of this is your personal credit stays separate from your business and if something were to go wrong you could re-establish corporate credit much easier than trying to re-establish personal credit. Lastly never sign a corporate check without putting your title under your signature. An attorney will tell you that if you sign with your title under your signature you sign as an "officer" of the company.

In the future if you are sued by a vendor you paid by check they cannot sue you personally by piercing the corporate veil. Use the same practice for contracts and agreements. Sign and put under your signature "CEO" or whatever your title is.

Q. What advice should I give to my kids when they want a car or credit card?

A. You have two choices on this one. First you have the option of giving them a duplicate card of yours and seeing to it that their portion of the bill comes to you. This will avoid your credit being hurt if they can't pay or you'll at least be forewarned. The same applies to automobiles. You can buy or lease the car yourself and simply list them with the insurance agency as a second driver.

Remember; make sure if everything goes wrong, you can afford to pay for your credit lines and theirs. For the record I built my first car from the frame out (1969 Firebird) with my brother-in-law for $900.00. No loan for Mom and Dad to worry about. Just a thought.

Secondly you could help them establish credit for themselves. Credit card companies practically give cards away to college students and the auto industry has first time buyer programs aimed at the same market. Here you need to keep in mind if your child / young adult doesn't pay or tell you they can't, their credit will suffer long after their done going to school.

Remember even if you do this thinking you'll have the bills mailed to you instead of them and help them establish credit in their own name they can have the bills sent anywhere they want if they decide it's better you don't see where they spend the money.

My personal feelings on this is to give them an debit card for cash and a 3 - 5 year old car with no loan outstanding if you can afford it. It won't guarantee they won't apply anyway on their own but it should slow them down. The last thing a 20 - 25 year old needs is to come out of school with credit problems before they step into the real world.

Q. What about student loans, should we help our kids get one?

A. Most parents and budding college students don't know they can get most if not all of the money needed for college free if they know where to look. There are hundreds grants and scholarships available from corporations, organizations and of course federal as well as state government.

Have your child apply for every grant or scholarship they qualify for. It is much better to help them come out of college debt free than to sign a bunch of loans most young people have a hard time paying once they get out of school.

Remember if they can't pay the loans the government will take their tax refund money away every year until they loans are paid. If you account for the fees and interest they add on it could seriously inflate the debt. If you signed for the student loans on their behalf it could be your tax refund they start taking once the loans default. I refer you to the chapter on student loans where we discuss in detail programs for getting the loans forgiven, cancelled or consolidated.

FINAL TIPS AND REMINDERS – Critical Forget-Me-Nots

1) **If you are threatened with a lawsuit don't avoid it**. If you can afford an attorney get one. If you can't afford an attorney, at least file an answer within the allotted time frame. Don't miss the court date or hearing if one is set. If you do there will be a default judgment entered against you. If you call the opposing side before the court date you may be able to strike a deal that will not only be in both parties interest but will also keep the issue off your credit report.

2) **Never ever tell anyone any details about your personal life** (creditors, collection agents, credit bureaus etc.) They will record what you say in their computers and use it against you later. That's not paranoia, it's reality.

3) **Every six months get copies of all three of your credit reports** from Experian, Equifax and Trans Union. The inquiries you create will not show to future potential lenders. In addition you will be able to keep further inquiries to a minimum by using these reports to shop for cars, boats, houses, credit cards and then only when choosing who you wish to do business with do you let them pull one for themselves.

4) **Avoid co-signing for anything**; it only creates nightmares later down the line. Additional inquiries and financial liabilities are the last thing anyone needs. It also has a tendency to put undo strain on relationships. If you want to help someone you care about sign as "guarantor" not "co-applicant".

5) **Don't ever allow money to be the reason you lose someone close to you**. Money can be replaced, friends and family can't!

REBUILD YOUR CREDIT – Without Borrowing

Believe it or not it is possible to rebuild your credit without borrowing money. It is also possible to do so even when your credit is still bad. In fact, you can put positives on your credit report while filing a bankruptcy. This is important because once you reach your mid to upper twenties and beyond and you have cleared off all of the bad credit from your credit reports, if there are no positives remaining you will be considered by lenders as a "ghost".

A ghost is someone who as far as credit is concerned is invisible, nonexistent, lacking in the financial graces. So be smart, use one or all of the strategies in this book to put some positive mojo back into your credit life.

First let's dispel some myths about rebuilding credit. You should not use the "if I throw enough against the wall something will stick" theory. Meaning if you thought the proper way to rebuild your credit was to fill out lots of applications and hope the numbers work for you you're gravely mistaken. In almost all cases all you would accomplish would be to accumulate tons of inquiries and that can only work against you.

Secondly you will not be rebuilding your credit if you get duplicate cards from someone else. Just because someone was kind enough to get you a credit card through their account doesn't mean you get the credit for paying the bill. Even if you do pay the bill it will only reflect on their credit. The creditors only report on the primary card holder of a given account unless of course the account goes bad then you might get the pleasure of dealing with them yourself at least for a while.

You are not rebuilding your credit by getting a higher paying job or by accumulating some money in your bank account. Not that either one of those is a bad idea mind you. It just doesn't affect your credit report nor does paying debts off through consumer credit counseling or on your own once they've fallen into enemy hands.

There are only two ways to re-establish your credit and that's by procuring new positive credit or reviving old positive credit. What do I mean? Thank you for asking.

In many cases you may be able to get old creditors with whom you paid perfectly to re-report accounts which have been paid off and therefore have not been reported on for seven years. Interesting isn't it? The law says "adverse" information cannot remain on your report for more than seven years. It says nothing of positive credit yet the bureaus remove those accounts from your file.

Here is another painfully obvious piece of evidence indicating the system is designed to provide negative information. There is no reason your past good accounts should ever be removed other than to force you into a situation where you need to start all over.

This is another reason to pull your reports twice each year. If you have relatively recent copies and the bureau removes positive information you can use the most recent report showing those positive accounts to get them re-posted to your file(s). You would contact the bureaus and get a supervisor. This takes persuasion so be patient and polite. You can always use the sledge hammer later. You can also contact the old creditor who was reporting the positive information and request they continue to report it.

If you are going to re-establish by trying to obtain new credit be careful. If there is nothing showing on your credit reports at all it will be difficult to get new credit with major companies. You'll have to start small like a secured card or loan from a credit union. Credit Unions are more likely to give you a shot at a fresh start because you are not a customer; you're a "member". There is a difference. Remember if you go around applying everywhere trying to get new credit you'll accumulate inquiries on your credit reports. Your chances decrease once you have three or more recent inquiries. Your credit score is what creditors use to decide whether or not to extend credit to you. That decision is done almost instantly. If you are declined you get a letter. If you are approved you get new debt.

CREDIT SCORING – Score Calculation and Usage

What is a credit score? A credit score is a three digit number indicating how well you manage your finances. In particular how well you manage your credit accounts such as mortgages, car loans, credit cards, school loans and more. This number is so trusted in the United States and elsewhere that most companies have designed their internal system to approve or decline applications almost instantly based on it.

Your credit score or "FICO" score is a number based on five primary factors or pieces of your credit life. This process was created by a company called Fair Isaac Corporation back in the 1950s. In 2009 the company changed its name to FICO. The three major credit bureaus use FICO scores when creditors inquire about an applicant to give a quick and what they consider to be accurate snapshot of the credit worthiness of that person.

If you've pulled your credit scores in the past you might have been a bit surprised as to why they are all different. The reason for this is the credit score on a particular credit report is calculated using the data within that report. As mentioned earlier in this book each credit bureau shows your credit history differently because the creditors do not all report to all three of the major bureaus for all account types.

Your mortgage company will definitely report to all three bureaus but your car loan may not show on all three. Your American Express card will show on all but your credit union Visa card may not. This is another reason why the system is so messed up.

There is little if any consistency and yet everyone is making millions with it. For now just remember your score is critical to your ability to obtain credit. Scores range from 350 to 850 with 850 being as perfect as it gets. If you want a new revolving credit card you'll need a minimum score of 680 to get it. If you want the lowest interest rate on a new mortgage you'll need to be north of 700.

Each credit and creditor type has different requirements pertaining to credit scores. Some types of credit carry more weight percentage wise regarding your score. Here is a general breakdown of percentage of importance by category.

1) **Pay History** = 35% (The more recent the issue the more damage it does to your score. The more severe the issue (Bk, Judgments, Tax Liens, Charge Offs etc..) the more damage is done.

2) **Debt** = 30% (Credit Cards, Car Loans, Mortgages). Regarding credit cards; if you want your score to be higher you need your outstanding credit card debt to be 10% of the total available. Example - $20,000.00 in credit lines with $2,000 in outstanding balances.

3) **Time** = 15% - The older you and your accounts are the more they count towards your score. Good accounts dating back 5+ years are going to strengthen your score much more than new accounts.

4) **Diversity** = 10% - Shows you can manage different forms of credit successfully.

5) **Inquiries** = 10% - Many inquiries (because you applied for credit) over a short period of time indicate you may be experiencing financial difficulties and looking to leverage your way out.

Never apply for credit without first checking all three of your credit reports with scores. When you inquire on yourself you do no damage as that type of inquiry is considered a "soft" inquiry not seen by future creditors. By knowing your score before you apply you will avoid being turned down unnecessarily and potential embarrassment as well.

If you are applying for a credit card and your scores are above 700 you should be good to go. If below 700 you might want to look closely at your credit card balances. If the balances are more than 10% of the total available credit you can pay them down until they are under 10%. Once you do the score will go up quite a bit.

RAISING YOUR CREDIT SCORE – 100 Points in 24 Hours

There are only two potential ways to raise your credit score. The first is to pay down your revolving credit card balances. The second method is to get your credit card limits raised to create a greater gap between what you owe and what your report shows you can spend.

If your balances are more than 10% of the total credit lines available you should first pay down the balances or get the creditors to raise your limits to increase the gap between what is owed and what is available to 90% available. Your score can go up the next day once the gap is reset. To make it happen that fast you will need to call the bureaus and tell them you are applying for a car, mortgage or other credit type. Tell them your limits are higher than they show on the report or you paid the balances down and you need your report updated.

The bureau rep will call the creditors to validate the new limit or balance and update right away. Your score will therefore change as a result for the better.

Key Point - Try to avoid having your bank issue new credit cards when you request an increase. The result of a new card being issued is the old one shows on your credit report as paid off with a new card or more importantly a "new account" number reported for the larger credit limit. The fact it's new will be counterproductive to your goal of raising your score. What you want is for the bank to "raise" the limit on your current Visa or Master Card account number.

SAMPLE LETTERS

CREDIT WARFARE - LETTER #1
ITEMS BEING REPORTED INACCURATELY

Bureau Name
Consumer Relations Department
Address
City, State, Zip

Your Name
Address
City, State, Zip
Social Security#
Date of Birth

To Whom It May Concern,

The following items listed below are being reported
inaccurately. These accounts and events did not occur as is
being reported.

Please reinvestigate these accounts and update my credit
report to reflect my true credit history.

Creditor Name and Account Number
1)
2)
3)
4)

Please send me a corrected copy of my credit report once
completed.

Respectfully,
Your Name

CREDIT WARFARE - LETTER #2
ITEMS NOT BELONGING TO YOU

Bureau Name
Consumer Relations Department
Address
City, State, Zip

Your Name
Address
City, State, Zip
Social Security#
Date of Birth

To Whom It May Concern,

The following items appearing on my credit report do not belong to me. These accounts were obviously placed on my report in error.

Please reinvestigate these accounts and update my credit report to reflect my true credit history.

Creditor Name and Account Number
1)
2)
3)
4)

Please send me a corrected copy of my credit report once completed.

Respectfully,
Your Name

CREDIT WARFARE - LETTER #3
BEYOND THE STATUTE OF LIMITATIONS

Bureau Name
Consumer Relations Department
Address
City, State, Zip

Your Name
Address
City, State, Zip
Social Security#
Date of Birth

To Whom It May Concern,

The following items listed on my credit report are being reported beyond the statute of limitations in direct violation of 15 U.S.C. § 1681 Section 605. These events took place more than seven years ago and should be deleted. Please reinvestigate these accounts and update my credit report to reflect my true credit history.

Creditor Name and Account Number
    1)
    2)
    3)
    4)

Please send me a corrected copy of my credit report once completed.

Respectfully,
Your Name

CREDIT WARFARE - LETTER #4
ITEMS BELONGING TO FORMER SPOUSE

Bureau Name
Consumer Relations Department
Address
City, State, Zip

Your Name
Address
City, State, Zip
Social Security#
Date of Birth

To Whom It May Concern,

The following items listed on my credit report are being reported incorrectly. I never signed as a "co-applicant" or "applicant" on these accounts. The creditor has no application with my signature on it. Please reinvestigate these accounts and update my credit report to reflect my true credit history.

Creditor Name and Account Number
   1)
   2)
   3)
   4)

Please send me a corrected copy of my credit report once completed.

Respectfully,
Your Name

CREDIT WARFARE - LETTER #5
INQUIRIES

Bureau Name
Consumer Relations Department
Address
City, State, Zip

Your Name
Address
City, State, Zip
Social Security#
Date of Birth

To Whom It May Concern,

The following inquiries listed on my credit report are being reported in violation of 15 U.S.C. § 1681(Section 604). These inquiries were not authorized by me nor where they for any other permissible purpose or legitimate business need. Please reinvestigate and update my credit report.

Creditor Name and Account Number
   1)
   2)

Please send me a corrected copy of my credit report once completed.

Respectfully,
Your Name

CREDIT WARFARE - LETTER #6
LATE PAYMENTS

Bureau Name
Consumer Relations Department
Address
City, State, Zip

Your Name
Address
City, State, Zip
Social Security#
Date of Birth

To Whom It May Concern,

The following late payments listed on my credit report are being reported. These accounts were never paid late as is being reported.

Please reinvestigate these accounts and update my credit report to reflect my true credit history.

Creditor Name and Account Number
   1)

Please send me a corrected copy of my credit report once completed.

Respectfully,
Your Name

CREDIT WARFARE - LETTER #7
FRIVOLOUS OR IRRELEVANT

Bureau Name
Consumer Relations Department
Address
City, State, Zip

Your Name
Address
City, State, Zip
Social Security#
Date of Birth

To Whom It May Concern,

Your letter stating my request was denied because you believe it to be "frivolous and irrelevant" is without cause. "The mere presence of contradictory information in the file does not provide the CRA reasonable grounds to believe that the dispute by the consumer is "frivolous or irrelevant". I therefore expect you to reinvestigate these accounts and update my credit report to reflect my true credit history.

Creditor Name and Account Number
    1)

Please send me a corrected copy of my credit report once completed.

Respectfully,
Your Name

CREDIT WARFARE - LETTER #8
STUDENT LOAN DEFERRMENT OR DEFAULT

Bureau Name
Consumer Relations Department
Address
City, State, Zip

Your Name
Address
City, State, Zip
Social Security#
Date of Birth

To Whom It May Concern,

The following student loans listed on my credit report are being reported incorrectly. These student loans are being reported as in "default". They were deferred not defaulted. The deferment shows as well. Please update my credit report to reflect they were deferred not defaulted.

Creditor Name and Account Number
    1)

Please send me a corrected copy of my credit report once completed.

Respectfully,
Your Name

CREDIT WARFARE - LETTER #9
TAX LIENS (Option 1)

Bureau Name
Consumer Relations Department
Address
City, State, Zip

Your Name
Address
City, State, Zip
Social Security#
Date of Birth

To Whom It May Concern,

The following tax lien listed on my credit report is being reported in violation of 15 U.S.C. § 1681. There is no record of any lien in my name filed in my county. Please remove this lien and update my credit report to reflect my true credit history.

Tax Lien Case #

Please send me a corrected copy of my credit report once completed.

Respectfully,
Your Name

CREDIT WARFARE - LETTER #10
TAX LIENS (Options 2)

Bureau Name
Consumer Relations Department
Address
City, State, Zip

Your Name
Address
City, State, Zip
Social Security#
Date of Birth

To Whom It May Concern,

The following tax lien listed on my credit report is being reported in violation of 15 U.S.C. § 1681: 605(a3).This issue was "released" due to it being withdrawn by the IRS prior to a lien being filed or adjudicated. As you know in accordance with the relevant section only "paid" tax liens can be reported. Please reinvestigate and remove the tax lien notation from my credit file.

Tax Lien Case #

Please send me a corrected copy of my credit report once completed.

Respectfully,
Your Name

CREDIT WARFARE - LETTER #11
VALIDATION OF DEBT

From: Your Name
Date:
Re: Dispute of Alleged Debt
Account Number#

To Whom It May Concern,

Please be advised your letter indicating a debt is owed by me to _____ (creditor) for _____ (amount) is in dispute. In accordance with 15 U.S.C. § 1692 – 809(b) consider this letter a formal request for proof of this debt.

I request you send the following proofs of this debt.

1) Original Signed Contract
2) Any and all statements
3) Any and all copies of checks or payments received.
4) Any and all late notices regarding this alleged debt.
5) Copy / Accounting of the charges substantiating the alleged balance.

Additionally please do not contact me via telephone at my home or any other location. I would like all communication from this point forward done via mail.

Respectfully,
Your Name

CREDIT WARFARE - LETTER #12
REMOVAL REQUEST POST LETTER 11

Bureau Name
Your Name
Address / City, State, Zip
Social Security# /Date of Birth

To Whom It May Concern,

The following account(s) (below) listed on my credit report are being reported in violation of 15 U.S.C. § 1681 and 1692. These accounts were disputed directly with the creditor under 15 U.S.C. § 1692: 809(b) (copy of letter attached). The creditor (collector) did not comply. Accordingly any reporting of this debt is a violation of 15 U.S.C. § 1692: 807(8).

As you are aware 15 U.S.C. § 1692: 809(b) requires a debt collector to provide written validation of the debt upon request by the consumer. During this time they must also "cease collection of the debt". If they do not comply within the time frame any reporting of the debt thereafter is a violation of law. Accordingly I have attached the letter sent to the debt collector requesting proof hereto along with a copy of the certified return receipt from more than a month ago.

Let this letter serve as notice that these debts are now being reported illegally and should be removed from my credit report. I will wait 30 days for a corrected copy of my report.

Account(s) in question:

Respectfully,
Your Name

CREDIT WARFARE - LETTER #13
BANKRUPTCY (DISMISSED)

Bureau Name
Consumer Relations Department
Address
City, State, Zip

Your Name
Address
City, State, Zip
Social Security#
Date of Birth

To Whom It May Concern,

The following bankruptcy listed on my credit report is being reported in violation of 15 U.S.C. § 1681: 605(a)(1). The Bankruptcy was "dismissed" not withdrawn.

As you know the FCRA only allows the reporting of Bankruptcies from the "date of entry of the order for relief or the date of adjudication". There is no provision for the reporting of "dismissed" bankruptcies.

Please remove this item from my credit report and send corrected copy post haste.

Bankruptcy Case #

Respectfully,
Your Name

CREDIT WARFARE - LETTER #14
FOLLOW UP TO CREDITOR RE: NON-COMPLIANCE

Creditor or Collection Agency Name
Address, City, State, Zip
Account or Reference#

Your Name
Address, City, State, Zip

To Whom It May Concern,

On ____(date) I sent you a request for validation of the alleged debt listed below in accordance with 15 U.S.C. § 1692: 809(b). It has been more than 30 days since you received my request sent certified mail return receipt requested (copy attached. In accordance with 15 U.S.C. § 1692: 807(8) any further "communication" of this debt to any person is a violation of law.

Let this letter serve as notice that you have 10 days from the date of receipt of this letter to remove / delete any reporting of this account to any credit bureau you have previously notified of it. Failure to comply will do further damage to my reputation and will be pursued to the fullest extent of the law.

Your cooperation is appreciated and expected. Please notify me by regular mail when you have removed this item from any and all credit bureaus you reported to.

Account in question:

Respectfully,
Your Name

I. Government Resources:

a. Federal Register for the FCRA
   http://www.ftc.gov/os/2011/07/110720fcrareport.pdf
b. House Committee on Financial Services
   http://financialservices.house.gov/Contact/
c. Consumer Financial Protection Bureau
   http://www.consumerfinance.gov
d. Department of Housing and Urban Development
   http://portal.hud.gov/hudportal/HUD
e. Student Loans.gov – Federal Student Aid
   https://studentloans.gov
f. IRS.gov – Topic 201 – The Collection Process
   http://www.irs.gov/taxtopics/tc201.html

II. Legal Resources:

a. Fair Credit Reporting Act
   http://www.ftc.gov/os/statutes/fcradoc.pdf
b. Fair Debt Collection Practices Act
   www.ftc.gov/bcp/edu/pubs/consumer/credit/cre27.pdf
c. Fair and Accurate Credit Transactions Act
   http://www.gpo.gov/fdsys/pkg/PLAW-
   108publ159/pdf/PLAW-108publ159.pdf
d. Fair Credit Billing Act
   http://www.ftc.gov/os/statutes/fcb/fcb.pdf
e. Title 11 – Bankruptcy - U.S. Code
   http://uscode.house.gov/download/title_11.shtml
f. Civil Procedure by State (Cornell University)
   http://www.law.cornell.edu/wex/table_civil_procedure
g. Better Business Bureau – State Lemon Law List
   http://www.bbb.org/us/auto-line/state-lemon-law/
h. State Debt Collection Laws
   http://www.privacyrights.org/fs/fs27plus.htm#Florida

III. Relevant Case Law – FDCPA (Debt Collection)

a. *Bartlett v. Heibl*, 128 F.3d 497, 501 (7th Cir. 1997) (Posner, J.). Debt collector may continue collection activity during 30 day period unless debt is disputed by consumer. Thereafter collector must "cease collection" until validation is provided.

b. *Baker v. GC Services Corp.*, 677 F. 2d 775 (9th Cir. 1982) appellant violated the Fair Debt Collection Practices **Act**, 15 U.S.C. § 1692, by falsely threatening legal action and by failing to inform the debtor that he could dispute a portion of the debt.

c. **Heintz v. Jenkins.**, 514 US 291 – (Supreme Court 1995) The issue before us is whether the term "debt collector" in the Fair Debt Collection Practices Act, 91 Stat. 874, 15 U. S. C. §§ 1692-1692o (1988 ed. and Supp. V), applies to a lawyer who "regularly," *through litigation,* tries to collect consumer debts. The Court of Appeals for the Seventh Circuit held that it does. A debt collector **may Not** attempt to reduce a disputed claim to judgment without obtaining the verification required by Section 809(b).

d. *Nelson v. Select Financial Serv.*, Inc., 2006 U.S.Dist. LEXIS 42637 (E.D.Pa. 2006); *Gigli v. Palisades Collection*, L.L.C., 2008 U.S. Dist. LEXIS 62684 (M.D. Pa. Aug. 14, 2008). A debtor's failure to request validation does not waive any right the debtor might have to deny validity at a letter date, and telling a debtor that failing to respond will verify the validity of the debt violates FDCPA.

e. *Phath v. J. Scott Watson*, P.C., 2008 U.S. Dist. LEXIS 17563 (E.D. Pa. Mar. 7, 2008). The FDCPA does apply to litigation activities, including formal pleadings by attorneys

AUTHOR NOTES

1. **Personal Note** - I've walked this path personally and know what you are going through. It isn't pleasant and the task may seem daunting but if you follow through you'll come out the other side with your financial life in tact.

2. **Follow Up Books** - Credit Warfare is more than 1 book. It is a series designed to address all issues related to credit and debt collection for both individuals and businesses. The next installment is called *Credit Warfare – Combat Tactics* (for extremely difficult financial issues) due out September 2012, Followed by *Credit Warfare for Business, Credit Warfare - Business Combat Tactics, Credit Warfare for Parents and Credit Warfare for Attorneys.*

3. **Expectations** – Manage yours carefully. The collection calls and any collection attempts should stop quickly once you send letter 11 certified mail but don't stop there. Follow the rest of the plan and you'll be back on your feet before you know it.

4. **Communication** - We have a **Twitter account** (@CreditWarfare) and a **Facebook page** (/creditwarfare) as well as the www.creditwarfare.com web site where we post information and resources frequently. Lastly you can reach me through email (creditwarfare@gmail.com) Please keep the messages short as I get thousands. I do read them and try to respond to all.

5. **Live Events** – The Credit Warfare seminar series offers an opportunity for you to come and learn the nuances of handling your specific challenges in person so keep an eye on our Facebook page or web site for upcoming dates and locations.

Made in the USA
San Bernardino, CA
13 June 2013